MANAGED FUTURES
An Investor's Guide

WILEY FINANCE EDITIONS

MANAGED FUTURES: AN INVESTOR'S GUIDE
Beverly Chandler

NEURAL NETWORK TIME SERIES FORECASTING OF FINANCIAL
MARKETS
E. Michael Azoff

TRADING ON THE EDGE: NEURAL, GENETIC AND FUZZY SYSTEMS
FOR CHAOTIC FINANCIAL MARKETS
Guido J. Deboeck

FORECASTING FINANCIAL AND ECONOMIC CYCLES
Mike P. Niemira and Philip A. Klein

TRADER VIC II: ANALYTIC PRINCIPLES OF PROFESSIONAL
SPECULATION
Victor Sperandeo

GENETIC ALGORITHMS AND INVESTMENT STRATEGIES
Richard J. Bauer, Jr

UNDERSTANDING SWAPS
John F. Marshall and Kenneth R. Kapner

FRACTAL MARKET ANALYSIS: APPLYING CHAOS THEORY TO
INVESTMENT AND ECONOMICS
Edgar E. Peters

TRADING APPLICATIONS OF JAPANESE CANDLESTICK CHARTING
Gary S. Wagner and Brad L. Matheny

FIXED-INCOME ARBITRAGE
M. Anthony Wong

CORPORATE FINANCIAL DISTRESS AND BANKRUPTCY, 2ND EDITION
Edward I. Altman

TRADING FOR A LIVING
Dr Alexander Elder

OPTION MARKET MAKING
Allen J. Baird

THE DAY TRADER'S MANUAL
William F. Eng

THE NEW TECHNOLOGY OF FINANCIAL MANAGEMENT
Dimitris N. Chorafas

THE MATHEMATICS OF MONEY MANAGEMENT
Ralph Vince

continued on back endpaper

MANAGED FUTURES
An Investor's Guide

BEVERLY CHANDLER

Published in association with ▶ | *Managed Derivatives*

John Wiley & Sons
Chichester • New York • Brisbane • Toronto • Singapore

332.645
C45m

Published 1994 by John Wiley & Sons Ltd,
Baffins Lane, Chichester,
West Sussex PO19 1UD, England

Telephone National Chichester (0243) 779777
Telephone International (+44) 243 779777

Other Wiley Editorial Offices

John Wiley & Sons, Inc., 605 Third Avenue,
New York, NY 10158-0012, USA

Jacaranda Wiley Ltd, 33 Park Road, Milton,
Queensland 4064, Australia

John Wiley & Sons (Canada) Ltd, 22 Worcester Road,
Rexdale, Ontario M9W 1L1, Canada

John Wiley & Sons (SEA) Pte Ltd, 37 Jalan Pemimpin #05-04,
Block B, Union Industrial Building, Singapore 2057

Library of Congress Cataloging-in-Publication Data

Chandler, Beverly.
  Managed futures : an investor's guide / Beverly Chandler.
    p. cm. — (Wiley finance editions)
  "Published in association with Managed derivatives"—T.p.
  Includes bibliographical references and index.
  ISBN 0-471-94402-5 (cloth)
    1. Futures. 2. Futures—Europe. 3. Portfolio management.
  4. Portfolio management—Europe. I. Title. II. Series.
  HG6024.A3C484 1994
  332.64'5—dc20   93–43615
                                                        CIP

British Library Cataloguing in Publication Data

A catalogue record for this book is available from the British Library

ISBN 0-471-94402-5

Typeset in 10/12 Times from author's disks by Dobbie Typesetting Ltd, Tavistock, Devon
Printed and bound in Great Britain by Biddles Ltd, Guildford, Surrey

Contents

Preface   vii

Acknowledgements   xi

Abbreviations   xiii

PART ONE   EXPLAINING THE MANAGED FUTURES INDUSTRY

1 Introduction   3
2 How Futures and Options Work   11
3 The Evolution of Managed Futures Funds   17
4 The Case for Investing in Managed Futures—
  The Academic Debate   23
5 Structure, Participants and Charges in Funds   35
6 Finding and Evaluating Trading Advisers   49
7 Performance Measurement   55
8 Marketing Issues   67
9 Case Studies   85
10 The Outlook for Managed Futures Funds   99

PART TWO   REGULATION AND TAXATION

11 Regulation of Managed Futures Funds in Europe   105
12 Regulation of Managed Futures Funds in the Principal European
   Offshore Centres   139
13 Regulation of Managed Futures Funds in the US and Japan   143
14 Tax Implications for Managed Futures Funds in Europe   151

Appendix A   Rules for Trustees of Managed Futures Unit Trusts
             in the UK   165

Appendix B   Managed Futures and the UCITS Directive   167

Bibliography   169

Useful Contacts   171

Glossary   179

Directory of Europe's Futures and Options Exchanges   183

Index   191

Preface

There is increasing evidence that more European institutional fund managers are considering employing derivative and leveraged investments in their portfolios, either for hedging purposes or to fulfil tactical asset allocation strategies.

Having borne the burden of a high-risk and shady image for too long, futures and options, as part of the broader group of derivatives, at last seem to be gaining recognition as prudent investment tools in their own right. There are many who now believe that the 1990s will be the decade of the derivative in the way that the 1980s was the decade of the equity.

Only a couple of decades ago, institutional investors generally restricted their portfolios to bonds (preferably domestic) and property (preferably commercial), reserving equities for more speculative and risky investment. Now the arena in which they operate has substantially grown. They are trading in international currencies (Forex), global equities, Eurobonds, bonds and, of course, derivatives. In many cases, the institutional investors are now using futures, options, forward rate agreements (FRAs), currency forwards, swaps and other sophisticated vehicles to redefine a portfolio at a minute's notice and to limit its exposure to risk and downside market movements.

The future for fund managers and institutional investors holds more use for a quantitative approach to investment. In its loosest form, this is the reliance on a mathematical model to generate buy and sell signals, and a strict disciplinary approach to doing what the model says. Other investment techniques, which we will see more of, are sophisticated hedging and cross-trading techniques.

Derivative tools originally were used mostly by institutional investors or corporate treasurers with banks or firms active in the capital markets needing to protect their own books from risk. More recently derivative techniques have been adopted by managers of pension funds, insurance funds and funds whose eventual market is the retail sector.

Managed futures funds, rather than undertaking direct investment in futures and options, represent an attempt to bring order out of chaos in investment in the derivatives markets. The managed futures investor is investing in futures, options, and other derivative instruments in an effort to achieve above-average investment returns, rather than simple hedging, through the application of an active management or trading system to the derivative markets.

Managed futures programmes can range from simple index funds which track indices through using futures or options, to vast, computer-based technical trading systems which arrive at investment decisions through the assimilation of a wealth of economic or financial information.

Given the number of problems institutional fund managers face in being allowed to use derivatives in their investment strategies, managed futures systems, with their investment objectives, recognisable structures and clear investment pattern, offer a more flexible, efficient and, in some cases, cheaper route to the futures market for institutional investors.

For institutional investors who are considering the managed futures market for increasing their exposure to derivatives in their institutional portfolios, but have little practical knowledge of such a market, this book provides a detailed overview of its background and operation. In addition, the aim is to provide a comprehensive guide to the managed futures industry for professional investors whose companies are interested in launching a managed futures fund aimed at the retail or institutional investor.

It will be of use to practitioners both within and outside the sector across Europe, and the rest of the world, including:

• fund managers, both of institutional and retail funds;
• business development professionals within fund management groups or banks;
• services companies for the fund management industry, such as accountants, lawyers or marketing professionals.

The opening chapters of the book are designed to give the reader a broad introduction to futures and options and how they have developed over the years. This background also gives the European—or indeed simply the non-US investor—some idea of how powerful this industry is in the US, where all types of investor from the man in the street to the corporate treasurer of a Fortune 500 company has an active knowledge of the futures markets.

It explains managed futures funds and introduces the three original arguments in their favour, namely that they offer:

• the opportunity to make money on both falling and rising markets;
• diversification of a portfolio;
• negative or low correlation with other asset classes.

Following sections give the reader a full guide to the different structures of managed futures funds, whether they are private pools, collective investment schemes, managed accounts or limited companies. It is also here that the reader finds the difference in trading approaches between a fundamental, technical or discretionary analyst.

It also addresses the controversial problem of charges. The high cost of managed futures funds against other more traditional types of investment has long been a point of contention in the managed futures industry. Clearly, high fees do nothing but deter a potential investor — particularly one who is already approaching the field with some trepidation and a pre-conceived image of it as a risky casino where the odds are always in the proprietor's favour.

Performance measurement is another extremely important part of this growing industry. Until now there has been little standardisation of measurement techniques for managed futures and there is no industry-wide comprehensive index for the sector. It is here that the reader will find the summary of the Liffe report and its subsequent recommendations on the measurement of futures and options in a portfolio.

Finally, I have provided two case studies of existing managed futures funds. These profiles are based on real funds and are designed to show how the structures, fees and guarantees of managed futures funds work in practice.

The second half of this book is devoted to the taxation and legislative issues for managed futures funds in Europe, the main offshore centres, the US and Japan. The last two are offered largely for the purposes of comparison with Europe.

Here the reader will find the regulations for formation, trading and distribution of managed futures funds and the current status of taxation for such types of funds.

Acknowledgements

The author would like to thank the following people and companies for their help in writing and compiling this book.

Anthony Belchambers of the Futures and Options Association for reading the manuscript.

Eric Bettelheim of Rogers & Wells for help with the regulations in the US and Japan.

Martin Cornish of MW Cornish, Batty & Co. for help with the regulations in Europe and the offshore centres.

Iain Cullen of Simmons & Simmons for help with the regulations in Europe and the offshore centres.

David Elkin of Credit Lyonnais Rouse for help with case study of Fund A.

Cynthia Gayle and Susan Abbott of CGA Communications.

Sohail Jaffer of Citibank for help with case study of Fund B.

Tina Kane of Buchanan Communications for help with case study of Fund B.

Victor Levy of Arthur Andersen & Co. for help with the taxation chapter.

Diana Mckay of the European Fund Industry Directory for fund history in each European country.

Jeremy Parfitt and James Wilmot-Smith of GNI Fund Management for help with choosing and evaluating CTAs.

Trevor Robinson of Fidelity Investment Services Ltd for reading the manuscript.

Simon Rostron and John Parry of Rostron Parry for help with the marketing chapter and for detailing how futures and options work.

Abbreviations

ASSI	Act on the Supervision of Investment Institutions
CAD	Capital Adequacy Directive
CAPS	Combined Actuarial Performance Services
CBOT	The Chicago Board of Trade
CEA	The Commodity Exchange Act
CFL	The Commodity Fund Law
CFTC	The Commodities Futures Trading Commission
CLMS	Collateral and Leverage Monitoring System
CME	Chicago Mercantile Exchange
CNMV	Comision Nacional del Mercado de Valores
COB	The Commission des Opérations de Bourse
CPO	Commodity Pool Operators
CRB Index	Commodity Research Bureau Index
CTA	Commodity Trading Advisers
DFM	Derivatives Fund Manager
EIFAN	The European Independent Financial Agents Network
FASB	The Financial Accounting Standards Board
FCIMT	Fonds Commun d'intervention sur les Marchés à Terme
(FCP)	is known as a fonds commun d'intervention sur les marchés à terme (FCIMT)
FCM	Futures Commission Merchant
FCP	Fond Commun de Placement
FOA	The Futures and Options Association
Fofs	Futures and options funds
FRA	Forward Rate Agreements
FSC	The Financial Services Commission
FSD	Financial Services Department
FTA Index	Financial Times Actuaries Index

FTO	Foreign Transactions Office
GAAP	Generally Accepted Accounting Principles
Gfofs	Geared futures and options futures
GNMA	Government National Mortgage Association
GSCI	Goldman Sachs Commodity Index
IA	Investment Advisers
IC	Investment Companies
IFSC	International Financial Services Centre
IML	Luxembourg Monetary Institute
IMM	International Monetary Market
IPE	International Petroleum Exchange
JEC	Joint Exchange Committee
LCE	London Commodities Exchange
Liffe	London International Financial Futures Exchange
LME	London Metal Exchange
LTOM	London Traded Options Market
Maf	Multi-adviser funds
MAFF	Ministry of Agriculture, Forestry and Fisheries
Map	Multi-asset plan
Mars	Maximum asset return strategy
MITI	Ministry of International Trade and Industry
MLM Index	Mount Lucas Management Index
MOF	Ministry of Finance
MPT	Modern Portfolio Theory
NAPF	National Association of Pension Funds
NFA	National Futures Association
OTC	Over-The-Counter
PAP	Private Accounting Procedures
PPP	Principal Protection Programme
QEC	Qualified Eligible Client
QEP	Qualified Eligible Participant
RAP	Regulatory Accounting Procedures
SEC	Securities and Exchange Commission
SFA	Securities and Futures Authority
SICAF	Société d'investissement à Capital Fixe
SICAV	Société d'investissement à Capital Variable
SIM	Societa di Intermediazione Mobiliare
SMA	Securities Market Act
TAA	Tactical Asset Allocation
UCITS	The Undertakings for Collective Investment in Transferable Securities
UTA	Unit Trust Association
ZAP	Zero Accounting Procedures

PART ONE
EXPLAINING THE MANAGED FUTURES INDUSTRY

1
Introduction

The financial term 'derivative' is a generic term for any instrument which is based on an underlying financial instrument or commodity. The term covers, most commonly, futures and options contracts. For instance, a commodity future is an instrument derived from the commodity markets — the markets which operate for the purchase and sale of corn and other grains, metals, oil and so on. In the same way, an index option is derived from an index.

Confusingly, the name 'futures' is often used in an equally all-encompassing way, and certainly the term 'managed futures' covers the use of all types of derivative products. This report focuses predominantly on managed futures, meaning investment in futures and options instruments.

Despite the fact that this is an industry which is so strongly associated with creating risk, the roots and the principal use of the derivatives markets are, ironically, firmly in the business of protecting against risk.

THE ORIGINS OF THE INDUSTRY

And First There Was Grain . . .

Arguably, the origins of the futures industry stem from rice contracts in 16th-century Japan, where the landed classes raised money by selling rice in advance of delivery to the rice merchants. However, the modern origins of futures, certainly as an exchange-based industry, lie in the productive fields of the grain belt in the US in the first half of the last century and the cruel exigencies of supply and demand. Price fluctuations for grain were violently volatile which had a serious and noticeable effect on the economy by causing an increase in the price of food.

At harvest time in the last century, the prairie-based farmer hauled his wagon load of grain to Chicago, and once there hunted for a buyer — along with every other farmer who had hauled his wagon load of grain to Chicago. In the way of these things, the price went firmly down as the farmer was forced to accept whatever was offered for his crop—or worse as he was forced to watch it spoil and be dumped in Lake Michigan. Come the late spring and early summer, harvest stocks were used up, available grain was in great demand and short supply, and the wise grain merchant who still had supplies made a lot of money—while everybody else suffered.

Not surprisingly, bitter disputes flourished in this chaotic environment, while price fluctuations for grain were violently volatile. In turn, this had a much more serious, or certainly more recognisable effect, on the economy by causing an increase in the price of food.

The problem gradually became so serious that a group of Chicago businessmen decided to try to do something about it and in 1848, 82 merchants representing every important business interest in Chicago met above a flour store on South Water Street and founded the Chicago Board of Trade (CBOT).

The Constitution, written in 1848 stated that the aims of the CBOT were:

- to maintain a commercial exchange
- to promote uniformity in the customs and usages of merchants
- to inculcate principles of justice and equity to trade
- to facilitate the speedy adjustment of business disputes
- to acquire and disseminate valuable commercial and economic information
- generally to secure for its members the benefits of co-operation in the furtherance of their legitimate pursuits.

The Concept of 'To Arrive' Contracts

At this point, the commercial sector in Chicago—and indeed that in the City of London in the UK—was using a 'to arrive' contract more and more. This form of agreement was the forerunner of today's futures contract. It allowed agricultural buyers and sellers to specify delivery of a particular commodity at a predetermined later date at a price that was fixed at the time of the deal.

As futures contracts became more sophisticated, they created an increasingly protective barrier against erratic price movements and so reduced the farmer's or the grain merchant's exposure to risk. To arrive contracts became increasingly common in all types of commodity markets: corn, sugar, metals—gold, for instance—and so on.

Development of Derivatives in the UK

The history of derivatives in the UK can be dated back to the arrival of the first centralised commodities market, founded in 1565 by Sir Thomas Gresham and opened by Queen Elizabeth I. It was based in the Royal Exchange (which in 1982 became the first home to the London International Financial Futures Exchange, Liffe) and was run along similar lines to the Amsterdam Trade Centre in the Netherlands, which had opened a few years earlier. Each commodity had a different part of the Exchange from which to trade. Despite the Great Fire in 1666, during which the Exchange building burnt down, commodity trading flourished in the City taking to the coffee houses, while the Royal Exchange was being rebuilt.

Each coffee house became known for a different commodity or group of commodities. For instance, the modern London Commodities Exchange (LCE) came from the Virginian and Baltic coffee house, while the London Metal Exchange (LME) came from the Jerusalem coffee house.

These early markets were using spot trading methods and it is from these origins that, as occurred in the US, the more complicated forward markets arose.

The Formation of Exchanges

With the arrival of futures markets on both sides of the Atlantic and the development of their business came the formalisation of exchanges. It rapidly became clear that while one side might use these new instruments to lessen their risk, others could take on the risk and make, or lose, money.

As time moved on, the players in these developing markets became divided between those who wanted to lose risk (the hedgers) and those who were willing to take it on (the speculators). To quote Anthony Belchambers in the *British Derivative Markets Handbook* (available from the Futures and Options Association; see Useful Contacts, page 175 below):

> Increases in the spread of negotiation and the growing involvement of speculators created a need for a faster and more accurate means of registering contracts. As a result, existing exchanges went through a period of modernising their trading practices. At the same time, new exchanges emerged which were purpose-designed to facilitate the trading of these new contracts . . . The last ingredient of modern futures and options trading fell into place (in the UK) when, in 1888, an independent clearing facility was introduced in order to provide a system of guarantee against default. This became necessary because many contracts were now being traded anonymously through intermediaries. This new facility called the London Produce Clearing House (now the London Clearing House) not only guaranteed contracts against default, but provided additional services of registering and clearing out of the system equal and opposite contracts.
>
> Anthony Belchambers, *British Derivative Markets Handbook*

In the US, the futures markets of the fledgling CBOT and the newly formed Chicago Produce Exchange—which later became the Chicago Mercantile Exchange (CME)—developed into the arenas where the hedgers and speculators met to establish the future price of a range of commodities, and later the future price of a large range of financial instruments.

The Arrival of the Financial Future

According to a key founder of the modern futures markets, Richard Sandor, one of the most important developments in futures was the arrival of the financial future.

> The greatest transformation in these markets occurred in the 1970s with the introduction of financial futures—foreign exchange and interest rates. The 1980s witnessed a second wave of innovation with the stock indices and options on futures, with interest rates now being the single largest component of all markets.
>
> A third major trend has been the internationalisation of financial futures markets. European and Japanese centres for futures trading have begun to occupy a major share of the international markets.
>
> Richard Sandor, *Futures & Options*, 1991

Throughout the opening decades of the 20th century, the futures industry flourished, spreading throughout the US and, to a lesser extent, in Europe, still deriving its business from traditional commodities.

However, it was not until the 1970s and the collapse in 1972 of the Bretton Woods Agreement, which had regulated international exchange rates since 1945, that financial futures arrived on the scene and the futures industry began to spread on an international scale.

Collapse of the Bretton Woods Agreement

Up to the First World War, the world's currencies were described either as hard or soft currencies, depending on whether they were convertible into gold at a fixed or floating exchange rate.

In 1945, after the Second World War, the Bretton Woods Agreement was reached and was responsible for keeping a narrow band of fluctuation (2 per cent) between the US dollar, which was pegged and convertible into gold, and other currencies.

By the 1970s it had become impossible to keep so many currencies, each from countries with completely different economic growth rates, within the agreement, and so in 1972 it was abandoned.

With the collapse of the agreement, foreign currency exchange rates were no longer fixed and could float freely. Belchambers outlines what happened next:

> This new freedom in the movement of exchange rates, coupled with substantial rises in property values, oil prices and the widespread printing of money to finance public

expenditure, led to substantial instability in the money markets and to double digit inflation and interest rates. Countries which had seen rapid trade growth suddenly plunged into recession led by an explosion of volatility in the 'price' of money. The climate was ripe for the introduction of 'financial' futures contracts. In 1970, the first such contract was introduced in the US in order to provide a hedging vehicle against fluctuating exchange rates. It failed. Nevertheless, the idea was taken up by the CME, which, in 1972, formed a subsidiary (IMM) for the trading of currency futures. On 20th October 1975, the CBOT introduced a futures contract on the Government National Mortgage Association (GNMA). Within a matter of months, the CME introduced a futures contract based on the ninety-day Treasury Bill. The CBOT followed with the launch of the most successful contract of all time, namely its US Treasury Bond futures contract. In the unstable environment of the 1970s, these new contracts proved an instant success and the concept was soon extended to equity indices.

Anthony Belchambers

Nowadays, financial futures products dominate trading over the more traditional commodity contracts worldwide.

International Development of the Derivatives Industry

Since the Second World War, the futures and options industry has seen massive growth on an international scale, with other countries coming in to challenge the US markets in their position as leading providers of futures and options.

This was clearly demonstrable in 1991 when turnover figures for worldwide exchanges showed the US markets experiencing a drop of 4.5 per cent in the volume of futures and options business, against an increase in the rest of the world of 16 per cent over 1992. Looking over the longer term, it has been estimated that over the past five years the percentage of business done in the US has gone down from 90 per cent to 50 per cent.

Although admittedly not a turnover figure which is typical of its day to day volumes, the volatility in the European currency markets through September 1992 made Liffe in London briefly the biggest exchange in the world by volume.

In the middle of the 1970s, the commodity futures industry was clearly divided among the main centres: Chicago for wheat, corn, soya beans and livestock; New York for gold; London for sugar, base metals, coffee and cocoa; and, to a lesser extent, Paris for sugar and coffee. By the mid and late 1980s, this was no longer the case. New futures markets were being established around the world, and the development of new technology ensured the wider distribution of price information. Meanwhile, restrictions imposed by regulatory requirements on cross-border trading or currency limitations were—and still are—being rewritten to allow for truly global financial trading. Finally, the natural international spread of expertise in futures trading had pushed the futures industry out from under the domination of the US and the UK and into the rest of the world.

Table 1.1   Top Futures Exchanges by Volume of Contracts Traded.*

Position	Exchange	1992	1991
1(1)	CBOT	150 030 460	139 437 140
2(2)	CME	134 238 555	108 128 604
3(4)	Liffe	65 872 355	38 583 877
4(5)	Matif	55 474 238	37 129 032
5(3)	Nymex	47 212 417	40 786 714
6(7)	BM&F	34 231 094	19 025 674
7(8)	LME	24 741 869	16 937 909
8(6)	Osaka	21 184 310	33 478 696
9(−)	SFE	17 557 685	12 496 050
10(10)	Tiffe	15 540 487	15 152 964

Source: *Futures & Options World Directory and Review*, 1993
*Includes only futures and futures options; excludes options on stocks and stock indices

Of the top 10 futures exchanges in 1992, measured by volume, the UK's Liffe and France's Matif now hold the third and fourth positions, while the remaining exchanges come from every corner of the world (see Table 1.1).

The highest new entry in this table in 1991 was the BM & F, the Bolsa Mercadorias & de Futuros of Brazil, whose option on the Brazilian stock index, the Bovespa, came in at position 20 in the 1991 list of top contracts by volume. BM & F was the fastest-growing futures exchange in 1991, with a volume rise of over 90 per cent on the year before.

The newer exchanges, outside the US, tend to be computer-based rather than using the open-outcry system that is still a feature of the CBOT and the CME.

Development of Over-the-counter Products

The international futures exchanges have seen massive growth over the last few years, but the over-the-counter (OTC) markets have seen an equally significant increase in business.

OTC derivatives contracts are tailor-made products which offer greater flexibility in return for greater cost, little regulatory protection and potential liquidity problems. They are generally used by institutions which have specific needs, for which exchange based contracts cannot provide, such as a French franc/Swedish krone cross rate or, indeed, specific interest rate date requirements.

THE GROUP OF THIRTY

The recent report by the Washington-based think-tank, the Group of Thirty, sought to address many of the problems associated with the risk of over-the-counter derivative products. The Group of Thirty or G30 is a private group made up largely of the senior management of banks from all over the world and academics working in the field of economics.

The current members are:

Rt. Hon. Lord Richardson of Duntisbourne KG, honorary chairman

Paul Volcker, chairman, Group of Thirty, and chairman of James D Wolfensohn Inc.

Dr Pedro Aspe, Secretario de Hacienda y Credito Publico Mexico

Geoffrey Bell, executive secretary, Group of Thirty, and president of Geoffrey Bell & Company

Sir Roderick Carnegie, Hudson Conway Ltd, Australia

Richard Debs, advisory director, Morgan Stanley

Sr Guillermo de la Dehesa, Consejero Delegado, Banco Pastor

Professor Gerhard Fels, director, Institut der Deutschen Wirtschaft

Dr Jacob A. Frenkel, governor, The Bank of Israel

Dr Wilfried Guth, member of the supervisory board Deutsche Bank

Toyoo Gyohten, chairman, the Bank of Tokyo

John Heimann, treasurer, Group of Thirty, chairman of Global Financial Institutions, Merrill Lynch

Erik Hoffmeyer, chairman of the board of governors, Danmarks Nationalbank

Thomas S. Johnson, former president, Manufacturers Hanover

Professor Peter B. Kenen, director, International Finance Section, Department of Economics, Princeton University

Professor Paul Krugman, Professor of Economics, Massachusetts Institute of Technology

Yoh Kurosawa, president, the Industrial Bank of Japan

Jacques de Larosière, Le Gouverneur, Banque de France

Anthony Loehnis, director, J Rothschild International Assurance Holdings

Shijuro Ogata, senior advisor, Yamaichi Securities Co.

Sylvia Ostry, chairman, Centre for International Studies, the University of Toronto

Tommaso Padoa-Schioppa, deputy director general, Banca d'Italia

Karl Otto Pöhl, partner, Sal Oppenheim Junior & Cie

William Rhodes, vice chairman, Citibank

Sir William Ryrie, executive vice president, International Finance Corporation

Jean-Claude Trichet, directeur du Trésor, France

Rodney B. Wagner, vice chairman of the Board, JP Morgan

Dr Marina v. N. Whitman, distinguished professor of Business Administration and Public Policy, University of Michigan

The production of the G30 derivatives report was prompted by the concerns of legislators that systemic risk may be growing in the OTC sector. The report followed a survey conducted by Price Waterhouse on behalf of G30 of some 72 end-users of OTC products and 80 dealers. The original report showed no evidence that derivatives increased risk but that there were some clear areas for concern. The G30 report had 20 recommendations covering a wide range of subjects. The report says: 'These 20 recommendations are not necessarily the only means to good management. What they do offer is a benchmark against which participants can measure their own practices.'

In summary, the recommendations said that each dealer and end-user of derivatives should:

- Determine at the highest level of policy and decision making, the scope of its involvement in derivatives activities and policies to be applied.
- Value derivatives positions at market, at least for risk management purposes.
- Quantify its market risk under adverse market conditions against limits, perform stress simulations, and forecast cash investing and funding needs.
- Assess the credit risk arising from derivatives activities based on frequent measures of current and potential exposure against credit limits.
- Reduce credit risk by broadening the use of multi-product master agreements with close-out netting provisions, and by working with other participants to ensure legal enforceability of derivatives transactions within and across jurisdictions.
- Establish market and credit risk management functions with clear authority, independent of the dealing function.
- Authorise only professionals with the requisite skills and experience to transact and manage the risks, as well as to process, report, control and audit derivatives activities.
- Establish management information systems sophisticated enough to measure, manage and report the risks of derivatives activities in a timely and precise manner.
- Voluntarily adopt accounting and disclosure practices for international harmonisation, and greater transparency, pending the arrival of international standards.

Beyond the recommendations there were four separate proposals aimed at legislators, regulators and industry supervisors. This group of managers was called to:

- Recognise close-out netting arrangements and amend the Basle Accord to reflect their benefits in bank capital regulations.
- Work with market participants to remove legal and regulatory uncertainties regarding derivatives.
- Amend tax regulations that disadvantage the economic use of derivatives.
- Provide comprehensive and consistent guidance on accounting and reporting of derivatives and other financial instruments.

2
How Futures
and Options Work

The point of this chapter is to explain very simply how futures and options work and how they are used. This is a very basic definition of their use, written with the intention of acting as an introduction to the theory of trading, rather than as a specific guide. The piece is written for the individual for clarification only — not to encourage inexperienced speculators!

The reader will find at the end of this chapter some more specific examples of how a company could use derivatives to protect against risk or to enhance profits.

HOW OPTIONS WORK

Taking as an example of options a share option; the purchase of an option is the right but not the obligation to buy or sell a specific number of shares within a fixed time period at a price that is stipulated when the option is bought. The sale offers the purchaser the right but not the obligation to exercise but commits the seller to fulfil those functions.

Example of Options in Practice

In August, you decide that shares in MF PLC will rise over the next month or so. The current price is 100p, and you hope that the shares will be at 150p by the end of October.

If you buy the shares, say 10 000 shares for £10 000 and you are correct in your expectations, your 10 000 shares will be worth £15 000 within three months, showing a profit to you of £5000, 50 per cent of your original outlay—less expenses. However, the drawbacks are that you need the original £10 000 to do this, and having done it and bought the shares, if MF PLC collapses in a heap and its share price drops, you have lost your cash.

As an alternative, you could buy an option on the share for, as an example, a 10p premium. This option would give you the right to buy a share in MF PLC for 100p at any time over the next three months. If MF's share price remains at 100p, you have an option with no value and so you have lost the 10p premium per share that you paid, and that is the extent of your potential loss—£1000. But, if the share price does go up to 150p, then your option has value and is certainly worth exercising, because you have the right to buy something at 100p which is currently priced at 150p. If you had just bought the shares and the price had gone up to 150p, you would have made £5000. Having bought the option at a cost of £1000 and exercised it when the share price hit 150p, you still make £5000 but you have to allow for the cost of the option. So, you are only £4000 ahead, but on an outlay of £1000 this is a pretty hefty profit of 400 per cent.

On the other side of this arrangement, there was someone who disagreed with you on what the share price of MF PLC was going to do. He took the view that the share price was less volatile and so it was worth his while to receive an additional 10p of income (beyond the dividends) in his portfolio of shares— assuming he has one. In this case, he could have written an option at 10p per share, which is the option that you bought. If the shares fell below 100p, the option would not be exercised and he would keep the premium.

However, if the price rose to over 100p and the option was exercised, then he would be required to part with his shares in MF PLC at 100p, or buy them for onward delivery at the prevailing market price. (Exercising, rather than trading, an option in commodities, is uncommon, but useful for this example.) However, he would get the 10p premium as well, so he would really be getting 110p a share, and this 10p would limit the paper loss in his portfolio if the MF PLC share price falls.

Buyers of options always know exactly what sums of money are at risk because they simply pay for the option. It is important to remember that the potential losses for writers of options are infinite although in the case of writers of puts— the right to sell an option—losses are limited by the price differential between the strike price—the price at which the option is struck at the outset—and zero.

HOW FUTURES WORK

A futures contract is a contract for delivery of a standard package of a standard commodity or financial instrument at a specific date and place in the future but at a price which is agreed when the contract is taken out. Certain futures contracts, such as on stock indices, are nowadays settled in cash on the price differentials, because clearly delivery of this particular commodity would be difficult, and sometimes, as in the case of the Eurodollar, impossible.

Example of Futures in Practice

Taking wheat as an example, assume that the price is £100 per ton today, while the price of a ton of wheat to be delivered in three months' time, is £110. The processor who buys grain decides that this is reasonable. He could either buy his physical wheat forward now, or he could hang back from that transaction and buy futures instead. He buys futures at £110. Having done so, he can now also commit himself to selling the processed product forward at a known fixed price.

Then assume the harvest fails and wheat prices rise dramatically, to £150 per ton. The processor, like everyone else in the market, will have to buy his physical wheat at higher prices. But he is hedged—he has also bought wheat futures at £110. Futures markets will now reflect physical market conditions and be trading at, for example, £160. Having bought futures at £110 he will now sell these at £160, ensuring that the higher cost of his physical purchase is offset by gains on his futures contract.

MARGIN PAYMENTS AND GEARING

Trading on futures markets is undertaken using margin payments. The initial margin is a relatively small deposit (around 5 per cent of the total contract value with variation margin payable on a daily basis). The reason for this is that it encourages hedgers to use the markets as described above without tying up large amounts of working capital.

The corollary is that the margin system also provides gearing, which attracts speculators. Speculation in futures markets is necessary for two reasons: first, it provides liquidity and turnover in the markets which make them more efficient and eases out peaks and troughs; and secondly, it attracts buyers of risk, which are the counterparties to sellers of risk, or hedgers.

The Concept of Gearing

Both options and futures markets are geared. Taking 5 per cent as a margin payment, that £5 per ton initial margin for buying one ton of wheat futures at £110 can turn into a substantially greater loss or gain if there is a big move in the market. Unlike options, where the premium is the maximum which can be lost, futures traders can lose more than their original investment.

If wheat futures fell to £100 per ton, then the buyer would lose £10 for every ton he had bought. If prices rose to £160 then that £5 per ton 'investment' generates a profit of £45.

DIFFERENCES BETWEEN FUTURES AND OPTIONS

The key difference between futures and options is that the former involve obligations, whereas the latter confer rights. Futures are a contractual obligation to buy and sell at an agreed price at a future date. The contract terms are standardised by futures exchanges, and the obligation, from both buyer and seller, is confirmed when the initial margin, or deposit, changes hands.

An option does not carry the same obligations. Buyers pay a premium for the right to purchase (or sell, in the case of put options) an agreed quantity of some underlying asset by a future date. The option buyer then has a further decision to make, which is that of exercising his option if he chooses to buy the underlying asset. In most cases, however, he will take whatever profit there is available by selling his option back at a higher price (this is why they are known as traded options).

The futures contract margin is, therefore, the basis of a contractual commitment, while the option premium represents the purchase of exercisable rights. In both, the concept of gearing is crucial, although there are differences. Option premiums are a wasting asset, and are much affected by the volatility of the underlying price. Futures margins are not a wasting asset and are affected differently by volatility. These key variations cause important differences in the risk/reward relationships involved in investing in either futures or options.

THE USE OF FUTURES BY INSTITUTIONS

The following examples are drawn from a booklet entitled *A World Marketplace* (available from the CME in Chicago and London; see Useful Contacts, page 173 below) and explain how a financial company and a US manufacturer would use the futures markets for diversification and hedging against risk.

> A major financial institution, anticipating a rise in the stock-market, wants to purchase a diversified portfolio of stocks with cash it will receive in three months.
> In order to lock into the current stock-market prices, the company decides to buy Standard & Poor's (S&P) 500 futures contracts.
> Three months pass. With the necessary funds now available, the company is ready to sell the futures contracts and buy the underlying stocks. As stock prices have indeed risen, the purchase price for the same group of stocks in the cash market is higher

than it had been three months earlier. But the value of the S&P contracts has also appreciated, so the company is able to offset the price increase in the underlying stocks by selling its futures contracts at a profit.

So, by using the S&P 500 stock index futures market—when it lacked the cash to buy the actual stocks—the financial institution today enjoys the same favourable stock-market position that it had hoped to attain three months earlier.

If the financial company had not used futures in this example, it would have missed a major opportunity to make money. In the next example, the manufacturer would have actually lost money if he had not had futures to use.

A small US manufacturer agrees to ship DM 125 000 worth of goods to a German firm in three months' time. When payment is received, the manufacturer will convert the D-Marks into US dollars. But the manufacturer is worried, for it seems that the consensus among international economic analysts is that the value of the dollar will rise sharply during the ensuing three months.

To hedge against the risk of a weakened German currency, the manufacturer sells a D-Mark futures contract (for DM 125 000) for delivery in three months.

When payment is received three months later, the dollar has indeed surged and the value of the D-Mark has fallen. The manufacturer, which now must buy a D-Mark futures contract, makes a profit between the original sale price and the current purchase price. So even with a loss on the conversion of D-Marks to dollars in the spot market, the manufacturer still realises a net gain.

Clearly, in these examples the financial institution and the exporting manufacturer had little to lose because they owned the underlying asset as well as its derivative: the financial institution had the stock, the exporting manufacturer had the D-Marks.

However, a speculator or investor in the futures markets has no actual position in the related underlying asset. This increases significantly the level of risk in the transaction so that if you get it wrong, you can lose a lot of money and this loss may exceed your original premium or margin. This is partly why many futures investors prefer to invest in the derivatives markets through the managed futures route, where risk is taken into account as a participant in the trade and risk measurement and control is given the scientific treatment.

3
The Evolution of Managed Futures Funds

THE ORIGINS OF THE MANAGED FUTURES INDUSTRY

In 1949, Richard D. Donchian established what is believed to be the first managed commodity fund, Futures Inc., which was offered to the public in the US. This fund was traded until it was dissolved in the mid 1970s. Donchian was a broker at Hayden Stone and he applied a system to futures money management, based on the application of moving averages. Donchian's initiative was not taken up by a large number of fund managers in the US and consequently managed futures funds suffered a temporary lull in their development.

The next development was that in 1965, Dunn & Hargitt became the Commodity Trading Advisers (CTA) for a managed commodity account. According to Thomas Northcote's *Major Events in the History of the Managed Futures Industry*, the account was US$ 2000 and came under the direction of a non-broker CTA and traded at Lamson Brothers (now part of the Shearson Lehman Brothers Group). Says Northcote: 'One of the more anachronistic policies of the CTA was that no women could open an account.' The management fee was US$ 175 per year.

By 1967 Dunn & Hargitt had introduced the first commodity price database which enabled futures managers to create trading simulations based on different trading styles, commodities and quantitative approaches.

In 1969, Commodities Corporation was set up in Princeton, New Jersey by a group of investors including Helmut Weymar, Frank Vannerson, and Amos Hostetter. The company started as a commodity think-tank, according to Northcote. He reports that the firm started out with fundamental analysis and carried on to incorporate technical information as well as fundamental data in their investment decisions. The company developed and supported new traders, including Michael Marcus, Bruce Kovner and Willem Kookyer.

Originally it had US$ 2.5m under management, which was invested in the US commodity markets, using the fundamentally orientated theories of Paul Samuelson, who later went on to win the Nobel prize in economics. (By 1990, Commodities Corp, as it became known, had grown to become one of the largest firms in managed futures in the US, with US$ 800m under management in customer equity and US$ 240m in proprietary money.)

By 1971, academics and money managers in the US had fully resurrected many of the theories of Donchian and began to design funds investing in derivatives for either institutional or high net worth individual clients. The theories included diversification across a range of futures contracts, trend following over different time periods and the application of various mathematical theories. The managed futures industry, as we recognise it today, was born.

With that birth came the attention of a regulatory authority, the Commodities Futures Trading Commission (CFTC), which in 1975 started looking after the activities of 225 commodity trading advisers (CTAs) or commodity pool operators (CPOs). By 1983, this number had risen to over 3000 and the industry was set for a period of rapid growth.

Managed futures trading had begun to develop overseas by 1972. In that year, Ulrich Becker in Conti-Commodities' Hamburg office in Germany began trading customer money in a trend-following system on a discretionary basis. Eventually, he managed somewhere over US$ 3 million and became what is widely believed to be the first non-US-based CTA.

The early 1970s were a rich period for the development of managed futures. A number of events during those years caused violent volatility in all types of markets. The Arab oil embargo, the Arab/Israeli war, recession and Watergate plus climatic problems of drought and freezes proved to be meat and drink for CTAs active at this time. It was from this point onwards that the managed futures industry as we recognise it today was truly started.

THE SIZE OF THE MANAGED FUTURES INDUSTRY

The answer to the question of the size of the managed futures industry is not as simply found as one would have thought. In many cases, institutional investors who are most likely to be the biggest investors in managed futures in terms of size of funds, use the private pools route to putting their money into the market.

Private pools are exactly that—private. They are set up by, for instance, a Swiss bank simply to provide discreet access to the managed futures markets for their clients.

This makes it extremely difficult to estimate the amount of money under management worldwide in managed futures. Most estimates are based on the publicly available information referring to managed futures funds and put the total of money under management at somewhere between US$ 13bn and US$ 21bn worldwide in 1993. In 1980 this figure was put at about US$ 650m, so the industry has seen significant growth. Taking into account the effect of gearing, even US$ 13bn under management, at the worst case, means that the industry actually controls considerably more.

MANAGED FUTURES—PRUDENT ACCESS TO THE FUTURES MARKETS

Before the advent of managed futures funds in Europe, many European countries—but particularly the UK—suffered the attentions of unscrupulous and largely unregulated futures brokers. These unprofessional operators encouraged retail investors to open their own trading accounts, through which either the vicissitudes of the futures markets or the inflated nature of the brokers' fees usually managed to ensure that the investors lost most of their money. Many of these unregulated practitioners arrived in Europe from the US, where the strict regulatory regime established by the Securities and Exchange Commission (SEC) or the CFTC had chased them out. The UK and continental Europe also managed to grow a few of their own cowboys.

Gradually, the introduction of a stronger regulatory regime across Europe and the growth of well-regulated managed futures funds—supported by their trade associations—have largely pushed the cowboys out of the forefront of the industry and out of existence, or into less well-regulated centres.

Unfortunately, however, mud sticks, and the futures industry has not managed entirely to recover from such bad press in its infancy. Much of the antipathy towards managed futures in Europe stems from this early history and despite the industry's best attempts and the wealth of academic evidence that managed futures do have their role to play in modern investment, there remain some in the investment community who will not yet consider derivatives or any type of leverage investment as a viable investment class for institutional money.

THE PRIVATE INVESTOR

Managed futures funds offer the safest mode of entry into the difficult and volatile international futures markets for the private investor. In their book *Futures Fund Management*, Nicola Meaden and Mark Fox-Andrews, both practitioners in the managed futures industry, state that

. . . the chances of an individual investor speculating in the markets independently and making significant money on an ongoing basis are probably less than 25 per cent. Most private traders are going to lose money.

Morton S. Baratz, the founder of Managed Account Reports (Mar) and a major figure in managed futures, agrees:

> It is received wisdom in the commodities business that 80–95 per cent of all individuals who manage their own accounts lose money in the markets. Just where that pair of figures comes from, and how accurate either is, is unclear. Each of the three careful inquires we know about puts the figure below 80 per cent. Blair Stewart in 1949, using data covering 1924–32, concluded that about 75 per cent of some 8800 individuals trading for their own accounts were net losers. T. A. Hieronymus, analyzing trading records for 462 individual speculators during 1969, put the fraction of net losers at 65 per cent. And R. J. Teweles and others concluded in 1974 that 'the average expectation of a trader [of] making profits in any given year will be one in four'.
>
> Morton S. Baratz, *The Investor's Guide to Futures Money Management*

Whatever the actual figure is, it is clearly too high for most private investors. The reasons for a high proportion of losses on an individual account are fairly obvious on the surface. For instance, it is likely that the individual speculator will have significantly limited capital, which means that an investment policy cannot be sustained through the inevitable periods of loss.

As small participants in a large market, individual speculators are also unlikely to have easy access to the best of commission deals on their brokerage business, and so will find that they are paying over the odds to participate in the business. They are also unlikely to have a complicated and tested system to apply to the markets and, most importantly, they are not in a position to be able to gather enough information to invest wisely.

Futures markets move violently because of a series of apparently unrelated events: during droughts, the appearance of a rain cloud in Nebraska could send the US grain markets into chaos, or a scandalous story about a country's premier could have a knock-on effect on that country's bond markets or equities. Observers of futures in early 1993 would have seen the effect of the substantial flooding in the US's Mid-West on grain prices, for instance.

The average investor does not have the time or the technology to collect together and distil all the information required to monitor the markets efficiently. In addition, speed of reaction to market news will inevitably be slower.

The Only Advantages for the Private Investor

However, the private investor does have two advantages in trading futures for his own account:

- Unlike the professional trader, the private investor does not have to trade if he does not like the look of a market.
- The private investor can choose which market he is going to trade in, again unlike a professional trader who probably has a seat on, at most, two exchanges. This limitation is gradually dissolving with the arrival of new technology and 24 hour global trading.

THE INSTITUTIONAL INVESTOR

Institutional investors are increasingly buying specialist expertise rather than developing their own futures investment strategies. In this way they can take advantage of the collective knowledge of the fund manager combined with the selection of a suitable manager and advisers chosen on the basis of past performance, trading history, and so on.

The basic arguments for investing in managed futures are that they provide:

- the opportunity to make money on falling as well as rising markets;
- diversification of a portfolio;
- above-average performance over the longer term;
- negative or low correlation with other asset classes.

There is a wealth of research and theoretical argument on the pros and cons of investing in managed futures. From this, two clear points emerge showing the strengths of managed futures over other asset classes. The first is diversification, the second (which is dealt with later) is performance.

Diversification

First, it is quite clear that managed futures have one major advantage over other more traditional investment classes and that is that an investment in managed futures increases the diversification of a traditional portfolio and so lessens the risk of loss.

Most portfolios, whether private or institutional, will be made up of bonds, equities and cash because portfolio managers have learnt, to their cost, not to put all their eggs in one basket. In the case of institutional investors, who are generally a fairly conservative bunch, the portfolio split will largely favour bonds over equities and cash.

The principal of portfolio diversification was turned into a science by the work in the 1950s of three economists, Harry Markowitz, Merton Miller and William Sharpe, who ultimately earned a Nobel prize in economics for their efforts.

4
The Case for Investing in Managed Futures— The Academic Debate

MODERN PORTFOLIO THEORY

Harry Markowitz, Merton Miller and William Sharpe were largely responsible for the work that collectively became known as modern portfolio theory (MPT). Their theories break down into three major parts: the efficient market hypothesis, the efficient capital markets theory and the capital asset pricing theory.

Dr Harry Markowitz started the research with his paper entitled 'Portfolio selection' published in the *Journal of Finance* in 1952. Within this paper, Markowitz demonstrated that diversification in a portfolio is only actually achieved when each part of the portfolio works differently from all the others. In 1959, he followed this work up with 'Portfolio selection: efficient diversification of investments', in which he elaborated on his theories of diversification.

The arguments central to Markowitz's work are that for portfolios to work efficiently, the investment manager needs to look at the composition of the whole portfolio rather than the careful selection of each part. Using a series of equations, Markowitz showed that a portfolio was diversified effectively only if each element within that portfolio was negatively correlated with the others.

Markowitz also debated the fact that investors are rational beings who know that they must make decisions with regard to the assumption of risk and expected reward. Investors, according to Markowitz, work with one of two objectives; either to maximise returns or to minimise risk. His work then turned to demonstrating that portfolios have theoretical levels of efficiency or natural points of balance. For any particular level of risk, he showed that there is a point where the yield could be optimised.

These theories produced what later became known as the portfolio's efficient frontier. Once the investor's preferences as a rational being have been quantified and slotted into a mathematical model, it is a simple step from that to identify the investor's optimal portfolios, as a point along the line that constitutes the efficient frontier.

This, propounded at a time when a clever investor was someone who could pick the right stocks, was revolutionary thinking. For the first time, someone was analysing risk in a portfolio, and beyond that showing that risk can be measured and managed effectively through prudent allocation of assets.

Markowitz's original work concentrated on equities and bonds and it was a long while before the MPT theories were applied to other investment classes.

THE LINTNER THEORY

In 1983 the Financial Analysts Federation invited Professor John Lintner of the Harvard Graduate School of Business to examine the potential of other investments to function as diversifying agents within traditional portfolios.

Lintner chose futures as the 'other investments' for his test study, a decision that was quite surprising as, at the time, futures were still considered by many to be too risky to take seriously as an investment class. His study, presented at the annual conference of the Financial Analysts Federation in May 1983, was called 'The potential role of managed commodity financial futures accounts (and/or funds) in portfolios of stocks and bonds', and has become one of the most important, and often quoted, works on the subject of managed futures.

Both practitioners in the managed futures industry and academics studying investment often refer to Lintner's study, which showed that Markowitz's model held up superbly with the introduction of managed futures. Markowitz's conclusions that careful selection, canny asset allocation and proper management were more important to a portfolio's performance than the particular riskiness of any particular investment were borne out by Lintner's work. He analysed performance data for managed futures from mid-1979 to the end of 1982—admittedly a short period for analysis—and discovered that the introduction of managed futures into a portfolio of stocks and bonds had a dramatic effect:

> The combined portfolios of stocks (or stocks and bonds) after including judicious investments in appropriately selected sub-portfolios of investments in managed futures accounts (or funds) show substantially less risk at every possible level of expected return than portfolios of stocks (or stocks and bonds) alone.

By the end of his paper he had reached the following conclusions:

> Indeed, the improvements from holding efficiently selected portfolios of managed accounts or funds are so large . . . and the correlations between the returns on the futures portfolios and those on the stock and bond portfolios are so surprisingly low (sometimes even negative) . . . that the return/risk trade-offs provided by augmented portfolios consisting partly of funds invested with appropriate groups of futures managers (or funds) combined with funds invested in portfolios of stocks alone (or in mixed portfolios of stocks and bonds), clearly dominate the trade-offs available from portfolios of stocks alone (or from portfolios of stocks and bonds). Moreover, they do so by very considerable margins.

Having made such an interesting start into the research of managed futures performance, Lintner's career was tragically cut short by his death in a car accident. However, his work has since been expanded and revised by other academics. The original paper was based upon data drawn from the composite performance of 15 trading advisers from a very short period, July 1979 to December 1982. This was largely because performance measurement in the futures fund industry was only just becoming a serious business itself.

PERFORMANCE

The managed futures industry is a very young industry and gaining enough perspective on its performance to satisfy the requirements of academic study is difficult, even now.

The researchers who pushed on with Lintner's work found that when they expanded the sample and changed the time periods or the computation of performance, Lintner's original theories were largely upheld.

For instance Mar undertook the research combining a portfolio of managed futures with a portfolio of stocks, a portfolio of bonds, an efficiently selected portfolio of stocks and bonds and an efficiently selected portfolio of stocks, bonds and treasury bills. The managed futures investments were looked at as futures trading advisers and futures funds/pools. The period of examination was January 1980 through December 1992. The conclusion drawn from the Mar study was that the inclusion of managed futures in a traditional portfolio of stocks, bonds and treasury bills consistently lowered the standard deviation for a given return.

Further studies of the effect of adding managed futures to a non-US investor portfolio showed that portfolios using managed futures performed better for a given level of risk than portfolios without managed futures. Beyond that, the study found that those portfolios that were hedged had significantly better results than those that were not hedged.

In 1989, Dr Carl C. Peters of A. O. Management presented a paper to the 12th Annual Commodities Law Institute in Chicago, entitled 'An academic perspective of performance in the managed futures industry', which effectively summarised the research results from roughly 20 articles and presentations on managed futures prepared from data compiled between 1975 and 1988. This work was later updated and republished in *Managed futures: performance, evaluation and analysis of commodity funds, pools and accounts*. All the following quotations from this work are reproduced by permission of Probus Publishing Company, Chicago, USA.

Each of the papers studied was given some type of independent reference and trade magazine or newspaper articles were specifically excluded from the 'evidence'.

Peters' paper asked five questions of the managed futures industry and reached the following conclusions:

How Does Performance Compare to Other Investments?

Here Peters looked at papers by Lintner, Almer Orr, Scott Irwin and B. Wade Brorsen, Morton S. Baratz and Warren Eresian, J. Austin Murphy and Edward J. Elton, Martin J. Gruber and Joel C. Rentzler who looked at the performance achieved by CTAs and public funds against stocks, bonds and treasury bills.

> The results were mixed. This is not surprising because with the exception of Brorsen and Irwin (1987), none of the research addressed the return-risk preferences of an investor. Managed futures, as a stand-alone investment, were found to produce higher returns than traditional equity investments, but with greater variability or risk. The answer of how good relative performance was, depends upon an investor's perspective.
>
> Brorsen and Irwin (1987) perhaps best sum up the consensus conclusion: managed futures as an independent investment performed better for investors who were willing to take on risk in order to achieve high return, but not as well for those who were risk neutral or risk averse.

These results do not apply to judging the merits of managed futures when used in combination with stocks and bonds. That question is addressed below.

Have Managed Futures Provided a Hedge Against Inflation?

Using the work of Zvi Bodie, Lintner, Orr, Irwin and Brorsen, Irwin and Diego Landa and Elton, Gruber and Rentzler, which covered data drawn from 1950 to 1987, Peters found a clear affirmative to this question.

> The answer is clearly 'yes' . . . all of the research results except one found that futures, and managed futures, performed better during periods of inflation. This confirms

the theoretical idea that inflation (and possibly deflation) should lead to patterns in futures prices, which should benefit trend-following CTAs who make up the majority of trading advisors. A caveat: managed futures were still in early infancy during the last period of sustained inflation (1979–1981), so these empirical results should be viewed with some caution.

Are Returns from Managed Futures Correlated with Those on Stocks and Bonds?

Peters found that none of the researchers whose work he was looking at had found any significant positive correlation between managed futures and stocks and bonds. Lintner found little or no correlation, as outlined above. Orr, studying the monthly returns for the Mar Futures Pool Index against the S&P 500 and the Salomon Bros. high-grade corporate bond index from 1980 to 1986, found slightly negative correlation between 1980 and 1983 and a slightly positive correlation between 1984 and 1986.

Irwin and Brorsen looked at the returns for 84 public futures funds and compared them with the S&P 500 and long term (20-year) US treasury bonds and found strong negative correlations between 1975 and 1984 on a quarterly basis.

Baratz and Eresian took the returns from 12 CTAs and compared them with the S&P 500 and US treasury bonds, using a weighted average of all bonds with maturities of 10 years or more, and found that between 1980 and 1985 there was little or no correlation. (Interestingly, Baratz and Eresian repeated the exercise roughly five years later, looking at returns from January 1984 through to December 1988 and found that the results were quite different. Through this time period, they found that in order to increase yield while maintaining a constant level of risk, more than half the portfolio, 52 per cent, had to be allocated to futures.)

Irwin and Landa studied the annual returns over a 10-year period from 1975 to 1985 from all actively traded public commodity funds compared with the S&P 500 and long-term (20-year) US treasury bonds and found strong negative correlation.

Elton, Gruber and Rentzler found no correlation between the returns from public commodity funds compared with the S&P 500, long-term government bonds, long term corporate bonds and small stocks.

Can Managed Futures Improve Performance of Stock and Bond Portfolios?

Peters found that most of the researchers he was looking at found evidence that managed futures could significantly improve portfolio performance.

Risk was reduced at all levels of return, and return levels were increased for all levels of risk, when managed futures were added. Investors would therefore have benefited, no matter their return-risk preferences.

Are Past Results a Good Indicator of Future Performance?

The research into performance predictability was fairly limited. Elton, Gruber and Rentzler had calculated Spearman's rank correlation coefficients for public commodity funds for five year-to-year transitions in rankings for the years 1979 to 1985 and found no short-term predictability.

They also compared the historic returns of public commodity fund prospectus information with the performance achieved after going public and found, again, no short-term predictability.

Franklin R. Edwards and Cindy Ma looked at the data for 55 commodity pools taking prospectus information showing performance for a 36-month period before going public and comparing it with the 24-month performance after going public and found no short-term predictability.

Peters says:

This is a good example of a bad question, and research (has produced) results that must be carefully qualified to be fully understood.

Are past results a reliable indicator of future performance? One would doubt this could be true over the short term. If it were, the best performing funds would, on the average, stay good forever (or until they expired), and the bad would do likewise. The same would hold for CTAs. Neither should one expect short term performance to be a reliable predictor of long term results. The search for predictability is in reality also a search for a profit opportunity, and market mechanisms are notorious for making such discovery very difficult.

Actual Performance

Over the longer term, managed futures funds achieve different returns from more traditional asset classes and in good years, managed futures achieve extremely good returns.

The following tables are drawn from statistics provided by the US Managed Futures Association.

The Spectre of Under-performance

In 1992, it was easy to forget that managed futures do achieve above-average performance: the industry saw one of its worst years so far, with average

Table 4.1 Comparison of Managed Futures Performance with other Asset Classes: % Returns[1].

Year	Managed Futures	US Stocks	International Bonds	US Bonds
1982	10.40	21.11	−4.62	31.10
1983	0.43	22.37	20.91	7.99
1984	21.22	6.11	5.02	15.02
1985	20.33	32.03	52.98	21.30
1986	−0.51	18.55	66.80	15.62
1987	60.97	5.23	23.19	2.29
1988	11.75	16.82	26.66	7.59
1989	4.79	31.52	9.23	14.23
1990	16.35	−3.18	−24.61	8.29
1991	11.50	30.57	11.00	16.13

[1]Table shows annual returns from 1982 to 1991, inclusive. Stocks return is measured by the S&P 500 index with dividends reinvested. Bonds return is measured by Shearson Lehman Hutton Government/Corporate Bonds Index (over one year) with coupons reinvested. International stock return is measured by Morgan Stanley Europe, Australia and Far East Index (EAFE-ND). Managed futures return is measured by the Mar Dollar-weighted CTA Index. Data provided by RXR Inc. (Stamford CT), Commodities Corporation (USA) (Princeton, NJ) and Mar (New York, NY).
Source: Managed Futures Association

Table 4.2 Comparison of Managed Futures Performance with Stocks and Bonds in the US 1982–1991: % Returns[1].

	Managed Futures	US Stocks	International Stocks	US Bonds
Compound Return	14.68	17.53	15.99	13.70

[1]Table shows compound average annual return from January 1982 to December 1991. Standards of measurement and data source are the same as for table 4.1.
Source: Managed Futures Association

performance for managed futures funds languishing at a loss of 7.90 per cent at the end of June. However, by September 1992, it was clear that generally June, July and August were good months, while the volatility of September's markets—particularly with the currency crisis—had caused havoc with performance figures generally.

The year before, 1991, was not a lot better, languishing over the year with lacklustre performance and then finally and suddenly putting on a spurt of performance in December. By 1993, performance had improved somewhat, with average CTA performance to August 1993 showing an increase of 15 per cent over the year, according to TASS Management. The key reason for this somewhat erratic performance pattern is that most CTAs are trend-followers

Table 4.3 Managed Futures Compound Average Annual Rates of Return Compared with other Asset Types (%)[1].

Type of Asset	Ten years	Five years	One year
Stocks	16.0	13.3	11.8
Old Master Paintings	15.8	23.4	6.5
Bonds	15.2	9.7	13.2
Mar CTA Index	14.0	12.2	7.1
Equity Weighted Mar CTA Index	12.9	15.7	10.3
Equity Weighted Mar Futures Pools Index	10.4	9.8	8.0
Treasury Bills (90 days)	8.8	7.0	7.1
Chinese Ceramics	8.1	15.1	3.6
Diamonds	6.4	10.2	0.0
House Prices	4.4	4.6	4.7
Mar Futures Funds Index	4.0	5.1	5.6
Foreign Exchange	3.8	5.4	0.2
Stamps	−0.7	−2.4	−7.7
US Farmland	−1.8	1.3	2.1
Gold	−2.9	1.0	−0.7
Oil	−5.9	8.5	20.7
Silver	−9.3	−4.8	−18.9

[1]Table shows compound returns for various types of assets from 1 June to 31 May for each time period from 1981 to 1991. Returns for asset denominations in managed futures are provided by Mar. All other returns provided by Salomon Brothers, New York.
Source: Managed Futures Association

and recently the markets have not been forming trends, tending rather to drift. This is explained more fully in later chapters.

The key point about performance in managed futures is that, in contrast to more traditional asset classes, performance can be achieved whether the underlying markets are going up or down. The clearest and most dramatic example of this is the period October/November 1987 when the world's equity markets collapsed. During these two months, Credit Lyonnais Rouse's Systemtrend fund achieved 14 per cent growth, and the managed futures industry's average performance was 60.97 per cent.

European Performance

There has, as yet, been little research into European CTAs as a separate phenomenon. However, Lois Peltz, managing editor of Mar, has undertaken some recent studies into the European managed futures industry and the CTAs covered by Mar's database, and has found some evidence that European traders have a low correlation with the Mar CTA Index. This is because:

- the time zone is excellent, allowing 24-hour global trading: early morning trading in Asia, mid-morning in Europe and the afternoon in the US;

Table 4.4 Mar's European Trading Adviser Index.

Company Name	Compound Rate of Return 01/93–06/93
A. K. Westphal (Winchester)	10.10
Adler Jansen Braun AG (Financial)	−5.12
Adler Jansen Braun AG (GLOBAL)	−14.03
Advanced Trading Strategies Ltd.	8.01
AHL Ltd.	6.97
Anglo Dutch (Currency)	26.67
Anglo Dutch (Energy)	−8.43
Ashley Levett (Winchester)	−4.07
Barry G Watson (Winchester)	−5.84
Capital Futures Mgt., S.A.	9.97
Chescor Ltd.	42.33
Comfitrade Inc. (Financial/Gold/Energy)	−23.75
Comfitrade Inc. (Currencies)	−15.62
Comfitrade Inc. (Diversified Long-Term)	3.35
Comfitrade Inc. (Diversified Short-Term)	−21.25
Commodity Associates BVBA	5.20
Copenhagen Asset MGT	17.92
Court Master & Co. Ltd. (Basic)	2.42
Court Master & Co. Ltd. (Metals)	2.55
Court Master & Co. Ltd. (NFP)	7.61
Court Master & Co. Ltd. (Options)	1.48
David Hunter	14.01
Dominion Futures Ltd.	7.86
Estlander & Ronnlund Mgd. Deriv.	−1.42
FFM Gestion et Recherche (Intl Bond)	5.85
FFM Gestion et Recherche (Softs)	−3.37
Folkes Asset Mgt. (Global Currency)	−0.72
Folkes Asset Mgt. (Global Finance)	−3.11
Forex Recherche	−13.05
Gandon Fund Mgt. (Currency)	10.19
Gandon Fund Mgt. (Global Financial)	9.67
Geo Economic Mgt. System	8.50
Gill Capital Mgt. System (Currency)	11.51
Gill Capital Mgt. (Diversified)	0.06
GNI Ltd. (Spread)	5.93
GNI Ltd. (Directional)	20.19
GNI Ltd. (Discretionary)	27.40
ITF Mgt. (Composite)	12.34
ITF Mgt. (Currency)	14.64
ITF Mgt. (Potentially Balanced)	0.32
ITF Mgt. (Potentially Balanced)	6.95
ITF Mgt. (Volatility Balanced)	4.53
John H. Harwood & Co.	−2.69
John Royden (ECU Cross Currency)	−6.59

continued overleaf

Table **4.4** *(continued)*

Company Name	Compound Rate of Return 01/93–06/93
John Royden (ECU Currency Options)	−6.55
Kingsfort Ltd.	12.19
Light Blue Trading (Bahamas) Ltd.	15.18
Mort Pty. Ltd.	28.11
Origo Valuta Styring A/S	6.75
Panholzer Advisory Corp.	0.46
R. Grace & Co. Ltd.	1.61
Riva Finance, S.A.	−3.03
Robert Hanna (ECU FTSE100 Options)	29.58
Sabre Fund Mgt. (David Beach)	3.00
Sabre Fund Mgt. (Diversified)	16.31
Sabre Fund Mgt. (Global Strategy)	10.58
Sabre Fund Mgt. Ltd. (Currency)	−3.16
Silver Knight Investment Mgt.	6.24
Sogemin Metals Ltd.	−0.73
U.B.A.F. Gestion (French Franc)	3.22
U.B.A.F. Gestion (US Dollar)	1.16
Winchester Asset Mgt. Ltd.	−2.33

Source: Managed Account Reports; reproduced by permission

- trading the non-US markets allows a more global orientation;
- currencies are a critical part of daily life for European traders who tend to have bank or brokerage experience; managing currencies correctly has a greater impact on European traders' results because when currencies are strong and trending it helps performance and vice versa;
- European traders are more focused on risk management because clients in Europe are less profit-orientated and more risk-conscious.

Mar has launched a European Trading Adviser index which currently tracks 60 European advisers. Performance over the first six months of 1993 showed a return of 2.42 per cent on money under management.

The European-based performance measurement firm, TASS Management has also looked at European CTAs, and found some evidence of growth in the numbers of CTAs. It reports that in January 1987, there were 11 European based CTAs with some US$ 35 million under management. By January 1989, TASS estimated that there were 21 CTAs with US$ 200 million under management. By January 1993, this had grown to some 65 CTAs with US$ 2.5 billion under management.

THE CASE AGAINST MANAGED FUTURES

The arguments against managed futures should also be addressed:

- their insularity;
- they are not an asset class in their own right;
- their high charging structure (see Chapter 5).

INSULARITY

One of the most interesting arguments presented against managed futures as an acceptable investment is that their development in the US simply reflects American insularity.

The theory is that having thoroughly exploited equities and bonds, US investors did not then move on and turn their attentions to the emerging markets of the Far East or South America in the way that European investors have. Instead, they looked at derivations of their own existing markets and came up with investing in commodity futures, a choice which led to the establishment of the managed futures industry.

The conclusion to this argument is that the derivatives markets are the US equivalent to emerging markets and that Europeans, not so limited by insularity, do not need to restrict themselves thus and can find more value in the emerging markets. It is an interesting argument but one that must be flawed. Derivatives markets are not just US-based any more and nowadays can hardly be described as insular, offering investment, as they do, in all the major capital markets and in the world's most traded commodities. Nor do the arguments of greater volatility and higher risk stand up against the emerging markets. The emerging markets have proved to be quite unstable investment fields themselves, with much the same degree of volatility in returns as those experienced by managed futures. Emerging markets are also expensive to invest in — and illiquid — and, in that the preferred route to investment in them is normally through equities, they offer little diversification of assets.

NOT AN ASSET CLASS IN THEIR OWN RIGHT

The whole question of whether or not managed futures are an asset class in their own right is one that can still cause a fierce debate. Within modern portfolio theory, the following characteristics of managed futures should mean that they are an individual asset class:

- managed futures can be traded to track an index;
- they can be used for passive management;

- they can provide expected return, standard deviation and correlations to
  other asset classes.

However, there are some equally clear characteristics of managed futures which
imply that they are not an individual asset class. They are not, for instance,
based on the same underlying assets; they are actively traded and do not present
returns when stripped of their active feature.

The debate is still open on whether or not managed futures are an independent
asset class, and certainly until there is a clear, industry-wide benchmark and
an indexing system for managed futures performance, there can be little
classification or performance measurement of them in their own right.

5
Structure, Participants and Charges in Funds

Put at its simplest, a managed futures fund is one where an investor hands over part of his investment capital to a fund manager who then arranges for it to be invested in the futures markets with the specific aim of achieving capital growth.

The basic arguments for investing in managed futures are:

- the opportunity to make money on falling and rising markets;
- diversification of a portfolio;
- negative or low correlation with other asset classes.

In the jargon of the futures industry, which is largely American in origin, the fund manager in this case is called the CPO (a commodity pool operator) and the actual adviser on the management of the money the CTA (commodity trading adviser). The CTA will advise on trading on the futures markets with the money under management. The framework of the fund and the expertise of the CTA are designed to manage the investment so as best to limit the risk of loss and improve the performance.

STRUCTURE OF THE FUNDS

Managed futures funds come in several different forms. If they are publicly offered, they are usually in the collective investment scheme form known as a mutual fund in the US, or a unit trust in the UK. They can be companies in the offshore centres, in which the investor buys shares, or they can be limited partnerships run as private pools. This last form is the one often used by institutional investors, who can commit a percentage of their funds under management to a private pool set up by, for example, a Swiss bank. Using this route, the institution can put money into the managed futures markets on a trial basis and in confidence, and can do it for less cost.

There is a further route to investing in managed futures, and that is through a managed futures account. For individuals, this is more commonly found in the US. Because of the perceived level of risk in these types of funds or pools of money, the minimum subscription is usually kept very high in an attempt to deter private investors with limited amounts of capital to invest.

More Complicated Fund Structures

Commodity pool operators have developed their own methods of putting funds together.

> New trading strategies derived from combining artificial intelligence, historical simulations and new applications of tested theory will also be incorporated into the markets. Mount Lucas Management Co. can test an algorithm using historical data going back 30 years. One Chicago proprietary trading firm uses 15 years of tick-by-tick trading data on key markets which are screened by artificial intelligence to discern price patterns over any possible time frame. These historical patterns are then compared against live trading data. Richmond Financial Resources, Richmond, Texas, has also developed an exclusively automated trading operation.
>
> Charles Epstein, *Managed Futures in the Institutional Portfolio*

The result is funds with nicknames such as Maf (multi-adviser funds), Map (multi-asset plan), Mars (maximum asset return strategy) and so on, and theories such as the arbitrage pricing theory (APT) which is briefly outlined below.

Multi-adviser Funds

The advantage of a multi-adviser fund is that the CPO can do a historical evaluation of the fund, taking the track record of each CTA, fitting them all together and showing that the advisers' performances negatively correlate but potentially can achieve substantially superior performance.

APT and Map/Mars

Multi-asset plan or maximum asset return strategy funds are more sophisticated again. The principle is one of dynamic asset allocation and the aim is that the fund will achieve a high proportion of the performance of the top performing asset—this fund should only lose money if all the assets were to go down. This is achieved by the creation of a synthetic option on the whole underlying portfolio which is, for example, a combination of assets and cash. This creates a cross-matrix of deltas of all the assets. A synthetic option is a portfolio in which the assets are held in such proportions that the price performance of the portfolio replicates the price performance of an option.

The easiest metaphor for explaining the Map/Mars concept is the one used by David Anderson of Allingham Anderson Roll Ross Ltd. Anderson uses the horse race metaphor, showing that a Mars fund is like backing all the horses in a race but with a bet which changes as the race is run: the aim is to achieve the average of the best, rather than the average of the average.

Mars is the invention of Michael Allingham, of Allingham Anderson Roll Ross Ltd. The Ross of this company is Stephen Ross, inventor of APT. Working with Richard Roll, the two academics said that shares are subject to systematic and idiosyncratic risks and identified systematic risk as of five different types: short-term inflation; long-term inflationary expectations; investor confidence; interest rates and the business cycle.

According to their research, systematic risks explain 25 per cent of individual price fluctuations and 97–99 per cent of the fluctuations of a large portfolio of at least 40 shares. The first Mars Fund emerged this year from Allingham Anderson Roll Ross, in partnership with Sabre Fund Management Ltd.

GUARANTEED FUNDS

It is generally believed that E D & F Man, one of the largest CPOs in this industry (certainly their partly owned CTA Mint was the first CTA to reach US$ 1 billion under management), was responsible for bringing to Europe what turned out to be one of the most useful marketing tools for the managed futures industry worldwide—the guaranteed fund.

The first publicly offered guaranteed fund was the Principal Guardian Futures Fund, put together by Index Futures and James Little in 1987.

A year later, Dean Witter raised one of the largest amounts of money for managed futures in the history of the industry with the offering for the Principal Guaranteed Fund, which raised US$ 531m, of which Dean Witter was forced to return over US$ 280m to investors, due to oversubscription.

The first guaranteed fund sold in Europe was set up by E D & F Man and its jointly owned Mint Investment Management Company. Mint Guaranteed Series A was launched in January 1986 and matured in December 1990. The unit price had increased from US$ 10 to US$ 24.49 over that period and the fund had US$ 12 830 648 still in it at maturity.

How Guaranteed Funds Work

The principle of the guaranteed fund is simple: the managed futures fund's capital is split, say 60/40 or 75/25, and the larger part of the capital is invested in high-grade securities, such as zero coupon bonds while the remaining, smaller part of the capital is invested in futures. The fund has a fixed lifespan, say five or seven years, over which the high grade securities mature, guaranteeing that the investor gets his original cash back, at the very least, or his original investment plus the returns on the managed futures part of the portfolio back, at the very best. The concept of a guarantee on the investment, a luxury that no equity or bond fund had been able to offer, revolutionised the market for managed futures.

To Guarantee or Not to Guarantee

However, there is a firm camp of detractors who do not like guaranteed funds because they feel that the investor gets such a limited exposure to the futures markets, with only 25 or 40 per cent invested in futures, that he may as well not bother. He is effectively investing in a geared bond fund.

   In the case study of a fund in Chapter 9, this problem has been tackled by the bank concerned who used a different type of guarantee structure which enabled more of the fund to be invested in futures.

PARTICIPANTS IN THE FUNDS

The CPO and the CTA

Most managed futures funds have a CPO, an institutional fund manager, who in setting up the fund appoints either one or a selection of CTAs who actually advise on the management of the money. Some funds have a trading manager as well, a specialist who advises the CPO on the selection of the CTAs. The number of CTAs used within a fund differs, largely depending on fashion. Multi-adviser funds were considered, for a long while, to achieve diversification of risk and lower volatility. Now the fashion is coming back to single adviser funds again as mathematical systems of trading become more complex. CPOs are also responsible for organising the back-office administration of a fund, the trustee and custodian functions, the marketing and sales of the fund and so on. While this is always extremely important in the working of a fund, it is particularly important in managed futures funds where supervision of margin or premium is essential to controlling a fund's exposure to risk.

Gregory C. Allen of Callan Associates Inc. (California) has published a very useful report on the subject of institutions using futures funds, *Managed Futures: An Institutional Investor's Primer*. His view on using a third party manager of managers is:

Due to the volatility associated with any single CTA, institutional investors have tended to shy away from single CTA programs in favour of portfolios made up of multiple CTAs. This approach generally involves the investor choosing a third party advisor (referred to as a Commodity Pool Operator or CPO) to construct a diversified management futures program for them.

This type of service is currently being offered (and actively marketed) by a number of organisations, many of whom are affiliated with large players in the institutional brokerage market. This approach can be packed in a limited partnership sort of arrangement or can be set up on a separate account basis. This approach has a number of advantages and a few potential disadvantages.

On the plus side, these CPO organisations typically have the database and the expertise to evaluate a broad range of CTAs and to construct a well-diversified portfolio. To the extent that the CPO organisation understands the specific strengths and weaknesses of the CTAs in their database, they can build a well-rounded program with competent representation in most major markets. Furthermore, a CPO with a thorough understanding of each CTA strategy can spot instances where the discipline is being inconsistently applied. This might lead the CPO to consider replacing the CTA to maintain the appropriate level of risk for the portfolio.

Another positive attribute of many CPO organisations is their strong back-office capability. A strong back-office is important for a number of reasons. First of all it allows the CPO to monitor the amount of leverage being used by each of the individual advisors as well as the total portfolio exposure to each market. By monitoring the total amount of leverage in place and the total exposure to each market, the CPO can control the potential risk of a large loss. Secondly, a strong back-office allows for effective daily reconciliation. Due to the number of trades that a typical CTA engages in each day, there is the potential for errors to arise in their execution and administration. The CPO can implement a daily reconciliation reporting process which will ensure that all parties are in agreement about which positions are open and which have been closed at the end of each day. A final reason for having a strong back-office is the need for competent cash management in these programs. Since the underlying CTAs use leverage to execute their transactions, this leaves the potential for a considerable amount of under-utilized cash in the portfolio. By monitoring the total portfolio positions, the CPO can get a handle on expected daily cash-flow and undertake a cash management strategy for the remaining assets. This can contribute significantly to the portfolio's total return.

Other companies involved in a fund often include a brokerage firm, which actually makes the trades at the exchanges. In the UK this is known as a futures broker or trader and in the US, a futures commission merchant (FCM).

Cash Management

There may also be an independent cash management programme in the fund. A CPO may either hire an independent consultant or use his bank to undertake a programme designed to increase the returns on the cash which is not on margin, that is not employed in the markets at any particular time. This may be as much as 80–85 per cent of funds under management.

In the US, and particularly in dollar based funds which most managed futures funds are, the low interest rate environment has encouraged the active management of cash. It is also becoming the case that the use of a cash management system is taken to be an indication that all potential profit areas in a fund are being addressed.

During 1991, several funds which had very bad performance found that using a cash management programme turned their performance from negative to positive — albeit a very small positive of one or two points. The psychological difference between a return of minus 1 and plus 1 needs no spelling out to the investor.

HOW CTAS WORK

It is, perhaps, because the commodity markets are so volatile and so erratic in their movements that they have attracted so many traders armed with higher degrees in advanced mathematics and technically complicated systems who are determined to draw a semblance of order from the chaos.

All CTAs trade using some system or another. Some employ superstition — trading on an equation computed on their mother's birth date or some other equally unscientific approach; some apply pure mathematics; some a wealth of historical research; others a gut reaction to what is happening in the markets; but all use some sort of consistency in their approach to achieve their results.

The appeal of making money in managed futures is the basic instinct that draws anyone who wants to turn a modest cash sum into a fortune, and do it overnight. However, the ability to manage money — and risk — in the futures markets requires genuine skill and is not common. Most traders lose on their trades more often than they gain. However, traders make money simply because when they do come out ahead, it more than makes up for all the losses. CTAs rely on a variety of routes to achieve short-term prediction of futures price movements. Roughly, they fall into two broad categories, the fundamental analysts and the technical analysts.

Fundamental Analysts

CTAs working on these principles attempt to predict the direction of futures prices through analysis of data which show the state of the underlying economic fundamentals.

By analysing fundamental economic data, the CTA hopes to arrive at some prediction of the supply and demand for futures contracts in any sector. For instance, a fundamental CTA who specialised in currency trading would analyse the currency markets, taking into account all the economic factors which move the value of currency, in order to assess which way the currency was going.

> A fundamental trader in Deutsch Mark futures would analyze such data as movements of West Germany's gross domestic product, its level of employment and domestic prices, its balance of international payments, and its interest-rate structure, in comparison with movements of the same variable for West Germany's trading partners and rivals. From this analysis, the fundamentalist will infer either that demand for marks is rising relative to supply, indicating a rise in the mark's price against other currencies; or that supply is rising relative to demand, suggesting a decline in the mark's value against other currencies; or little or no significant change in the relationship between supply and demand, indicating no change in the mark's external value.
>
> Baratz, *The Investor's Guide to Futures Money Management*

So, fundamental analysis is based on the belief that the free market is controlled by the forces of supply and demand, a belief that is not particularly revolutionary in the western world—or even much in the east, these days.

However, there are problems with this approach to analysing and predicting price movements in the futures markets. Political change or unrest, or that little rain cloud over Nebraska can have a dramatic effect on a market, making it look quite different from the one that the economic fundamentals might suggest.

It is also worth bearing in mind the fact that traders are human. According to Baratz: 'A second set of factors difficult to handle in a theoretical model is usually labelled behavioral and refers to the intestinal, as opposed to the intellectual, reactions of other futures traders.'

The common emotional experience is particularly a feature of the trading-floor based US exchanges where the open outcry system means that up to 600 dealers get squashed into a very small pit, in an effort to get a better deal than the next person. 'Intestinal reactions' undoubtedly do get passed around in this environment—at the very least—and it all contributes to price movements and yet all remains quite unquantifiable and outside the scope of fundamental economics. Admittedly, these are traders not CTAs but the effect must get carried down.

Finally, there is also the fact that fundamental information is available to everybody in a market, not just fundamental CTAs, and is likely to have already been taken into account by the market.

The second type of trader attempts to deal with these difficulties by leaving out the fundamentals altogether.

Technical Analysts

According to Baratz:

> Technical analysts finesse these difficulties by the simple device of ignoring the fundamentals. They accept as plain truth the contention of Charles Dow, an early

and vigorous proponent of what is now called technical analysis, that: the market reflects all the jobber knows about the conditions of the textile trade; all the banker knows about the money market; all that the best-informed president knows of his own business, together with his knowledge of all other businesses; it sees the general condition of transportation in a way that the president of no single railroad can ever see; it is better informed on crops than the farmer or even the Department of Agriculture. In fact, the market reduces to a bloodless verdict all knowledge bearing on finance, both domestic and foreign.

Technical analysts look for waves of activity in a market in order to get on to them at the beginning, be with them at the crest and, ideally, hop off on to a new wave before the first one crashes. They mostly focus on the short-term, recurring patterns of a market.

Technical analysts are usually reliant on their own highly complex proprietary computer systems which are based on econometric models covering information that spans from fundamental economic data to providing a historical perspective. The technical analyst attempts to take out all emotion and subjectivity from the trading process, believing that only by maintaining a disciplined approach to using a system can performance be achieved over the long term.

Discretionary Analysts

Other types of traders base their beliefs on the random and efficient markets theories. In these markets, systems are pointless, they argue, because if you stick with any system for long enough, it will finally come good. The problem is simply whether you can wait long enough for the market finally to match the investment. So these types of traders prefer to use charts or computer systems for research purposes only and override automated systems to make the final investment decisions themselves.

Market Wizards

Jack D. Schwager, director of Futures Research and Trading Strategy at Prudential Bache Securities in New York has written a very popular book based on research and interviews with successful traders in an effort to find out what they are doing right. In *Market Wizards: Interviews with Top Traders*, Schwager found that despite the fact that the approach in trading styles varies dramatically between types of traders, there were some features of trading which were common to all.

It is in Schwager's book that one finds the tales of extraordinary investment performance which encourage many investors to join in the futures markets. Schwager tells of a trader, Michael Marcus, who turned a US$ 30 000 account into US$ 80m over 10 years, after having been wiped out several times in his career; of Ed Seykota, who started a customer account in 1972 with US$ 5000 and was up 250 000 per cent by mid-1988, on a cash-on-cash basis. He also interviews Paul Tudor Jones, one of the best known of the US CTAs, who made 62 per cent in October 1987 and achieved five consecutive years of triple-digit returns through the 1980s.

These are extraordinary and uncommon feats, not the type of performance which can be easily achieved by many traders. The rules for trading as recommended by Seykota in the book are simple and contradictory:

- cut losses;
- ride winners;
- keep bets small;
- follow the rules without question;
- know when to break the rules.

Schwager finally concludes:

There is no holy grail to trading success. The methodologies employed by the 'market wizards' cover the entire spectrum from purely technical to purely fundamental — and everything in between. The length of time they typically hold a trade ranges from minutes to years. Although the styles of the traders are very different, many common denominators were evident:

1. All those interviewed had a driving desire to become successful traders — in many cases, overcoming significant obstacles to reach their goal.
2. All reflected confidence that they could continue to win over the long run. Almost invariably, they considered their own trading as the best and safest investment for their money.
3. Each trader had found a methodology that worked for him and remained true to that approach. It is significant that discipline was the word most frequently mentioned.
4. The top traders take their trading very seriously; most devote a substantial amount of their waking hours to market analysis and trading strategy.
5. Rigid risk control is one of the key elements in the trading strategy of virtually all those interviewed.
6. In a variety of ways, many of the traders stressed the importance of having the patience to wait for the right trading opportunity to present itself.
7. The importance of acting independently of the crowd was a frequently emphasized point.
8. All the top traders understand that losing is part of the game.
9. They all love what they are doing.

THE PROBLEM OF FEES

The cost of investing in managed futures funds is the most controversial problem for the industry—although, a more cynical interpretation from the point of view of institutions looking to launch managed futures funds must find the charging structure rather appealing, offering as it does great opportunities to make money for the fund management group.

Managed futures funds, accounts or pools carry very high fees. The standard fee structure is as follows:

- introductory commission, paid to an introducing intermediary;
- management fees, paid to the CPO and the CTA to cover administrative expenses;
- incentive fees, paid to the CTA in most cases (also known as the performance fee);
- transaction fees or brokerage commissions;
- early redemption fees, although these are only charged in retail funds in the US.

Introductory Commission

This type of fee on a fund in Europe can be represented either in a bid/offer spread on the fund's unit price, which means that the introductory commission is anything between 2 per cent and 8 per cent, or it can take the US mutual fund route and be charged at the back of the fund. If the money to cover this fee does not come out of the bid/offer spread, it is usually paid for out of the brokerage commission or management fees.

Management Fees

These charges are anything from 1 per cent to 6 per cent of the assets under management per annum and come straight out of the fund.

Incentive or Performance Fees

These are usually paid on a net new high basis and can be anywhere between 15 per cent and 30 per cent. Net new high means that if a CTA achieves a new high, over the old one, he gets a percentage of that new high profit. Some funds with multi-adviser structures limit the performance fee to only that part of the money that the CTA himself manages—so if a currency-based CTA achieves a net new high and no other CTA does, then just the currency orientated adviser gets the performance fee. This is known as the netting of performance fees. The question of how much of the fund is considered to be an asset also has a different answer in each quarter. Meaden and Fox-Andrews say:

> Other [concerns] are much more prickly indeed. Should the interest income earned on assets not allocated to trading be included in 'net new' profits for example? Some industry participants argue that it is outrageous for an investment manager to earn an incentive fee on interest income. Others argue that the manager who makes a deliberate decision to stay out of the markets for a time, has made a responsible investment decision and has every right to charge an incentive fee on interest income.

Incentive fees or brokerage commissions might appear to be the least controversial of the fees charged on funds, but it is in the small print in the prospectuses of these funds that the investor may find further drains upon the fund's resources. It is not uncommon, for instance, that fund managers who hire intermediary CPOs to organise the CTAs will charge a further lump sum fee annually against the fund.

Brokerage Commissions

These charges are usually quoted on a round turn basis, that is, representing the buy and sell process, and can vary significantly, from between US$ 15 and US$ 60 a round turn.

DEALING WITH THE FEES PROBLEM

Funds that are guaranteed carry more charges again, with a fee to the bank that is underwriting the guarantee, a fee for the zero coupon bonds or whichever high-grade security is being used for the guaranteed elements and so on. Clearly the institutional investor, for whom investing in futures is not the magical, mystical activity that it may be for the retail investor, is going to balk at paying these fees.

For their part, CTAs are generally not happy with high fees either, because it puts more of a strain on them to perform if up to 12 or 13 per cent of the money under management has disappeared in the first second that the fund starts trading. For some retail guaranteed funds, this is particularly important because these funds have high stop/loss points, which means that if the fund's capital drops by more than 15 per cent, for example, the fund has to be wound up. Obviously, this stop/loss point can be hit much more quickly if fees are high.

Allen says in *Managed Futures: An Institutional Investor's Primer* that:

There are two significant potential problems with a manager of managers program that bear mentioning. To the extent that these problems are monitored, they can be controlled. First of all is the issue of costs and fees. Commodity Pool Operators must pay fees to the individual CTAs. These fees are generally structured as a flat percentage of assets with an additional performance based component. The CPO will also typically tack on an additional charge for administering the program. Finally, to the extent that the CPO is associated with a brokerage operation they can require the underlying CTAs to direct brokerage through their organization. This triple tiered cost structure can create a significant drag on portfolio performance. On a percentage of assets under management basis, total costs for a managed futures program can exceed those associated with an institutional domestic equity portfolio by five to 20 times. Each component of this cost structure is to some extent negotiable. Proper due diligence will involve ensuring the most competitive total fee and cost structure for the desired level of service.

Allen, Managed Futures: An Institutional Investor's Primer

The second problem referred to by Allen is the difficulty of focusing on recent performance when selecting CTAs. This subject is dealt with in the next chapter.

According to the work of Frank Pusateri and John Stapleton, the level of commissions affects more than just the performance of a fund. Reporting this study in *Managed Futures Come of Age*, Epstein (1992) says:

> In a survey conducted by Pusateri and Stapleton (1990), trading advisors whose equity was raised by large brokerage firms had track records reflecting commissions in excess of US$ 50 per round turn. 'Substantial trading advisors' had commissions as high as US$ 80 to US$ 90 per round turn. These commission rates were significantly higher than traders who raised their own equity for client accounts and pools which had average commission rates of US$ 25 per round turn. The study showed some had commissions as low as US$ 15.
>
> By examining the commission rates and annual gross commission as a percentage of equity, Pusateri and Stapleton estimated the historical effect of a lower commission rate on an advisor's track record. They concluded that an advisor with a composite track record based on an average commission rate of US$ 75 (including 12 per cent of equity in annual commissions) would have increased their annual performance by 8 per cent if commissions were reduced to US$ 25 . . .

Pusateri and Stapleton's work also showed that rates of commission affect the risk-reward ratios in funds.

A recent study in *Managed Derivatives* magazine (see Useful Contacts, page 176 below, for details) showed that high fees cramp performance.

> Industry observers claim that the total effect of fee structures is to transfer almost all risk to the investor. This claim needs stating because it is a condition attached to futures funds which investors are finding less and less tolerable. With retail products the guaranteed funds have attempted to resolve this problem in terms of investor *perception* of risk, but for large institutional investors who can hedge their own risk, these fees are too high a price to pay for exposure to leverage.
>
> Funds which recently described themselves as ''changing the relationship between risk and reward in favour of the investor'' do so through more sophisticated risk

Table 5.1 Breakdown of Fund Charges—Sample of 142 from the TASS Database to end May 1993.

Management charges:									
Range %	0	>0-0.9	1-1.9	2-2.9	3-3.9	4-4.9	5-5.9	6-6.9	>7
Management %	9.7	1.4	6.9	21.4	23.4	16.6	2.8	15.2	2.8
Incentive charges:									
Range %	0	>0-5	6-10	11-15	16-20	21-25	26-30	>30	
Incentive %	5.6	0.7	0.7	35.2	40.8	14.1	2.1	0.7	
Charges on sales:									
Range %	0	>0-9	1-1.9	2-2.9	3-3.9	4-4.9	5-5.9	6-6.7	>7
Sales %	72.9	0.7	1.5	3.6	8.0	5.1	6.6	0.7	0.7

Source: Managed Derivatives.

control program — in reality of course, the investor still bears the burden of financial losses.

This situation is further agitated by the use of brokerage charges as profit centres by fund managers. There is a premium put on the actual costs of financial transactions (believed to be as low as US$ 3–4 per round-turn) so a charge on round-turns which can encourage CTAs to churn portfolios to generate brokerage fees — especially when these are directed back to the fund manager's own broking facility or subsidiary. Mar calculates that the average number of round-turns performed by a CTA to June this year was 2,597 round-turns/US$m/year and a commission to equity (proportion of funds under management which brokerage fees represent) of 6.2 per cent. This figure can be manipulated massively by raising or lowering brokerage fees.

At this number of round-turns charged at US$ 15, a fully-traded fund of US$ 30m will earn a very reasonable 4 per cent commission to equity, but increasing the volume of trades will increase this figure by a proportional amount. And US$ 60 per round-turn, by no means an unusually high charge, will produce 16 per cent commission to equity. Presumably, such high fees will indicate a lesser number of round turns, but the investor cannot bank on it.

Katy Massey, *Managed Derivatives*

Some comfort for the institutional investor may come from the knowledge that the fee structure for these funds is changing. A major innovation in 1991 was the launch of the Investor's Advantage Fund LP, which back-loaded all management and performance fees so that all fees were performance based. The fund was structured so that all management fees are paid out after the customer has received 100 per cent of the prevailing treasury bill rate.

Managed futures are a very specialist investment field and accordingly investors should expect to pay a slightly higher fee. However, there is a middle ground and that has certainly not been reached by many of the fund management groups running such funds in Europe at the moment.

However, many of the criticisms hurled at managed futures funds for their high level of charging are unjustified if compared to the level of hidden costs in more familiar funds such as general unit trusts, mutual funds or the UK's investment trusts.

Managed futures will undoubtedly do themselves a great favour by coming up with a cheaper structure. The industry must welcome any initiatives to cut costs, such as that of the Investor's Advantage Fund. To the outside observer, it also does not seem clear why there are not more examples of a CTA launching his own fund, thereby skipping one layer of this industry by leaving out the CPO and the CPO's charges: maybe in the future more CPOs will buy CTAs and take them in-house or CTAs will launch more funds in their own right. Companies such as E D & F Man (owners of Adam, Harding & Lueck) have done exactly that — maybe more will join them.

6
Finding and Evaluating Trading Advisers

DEMOGRAPHIC CHANGE AND AGEING POPULATIONS

In Europe as a whole, one of the greatest features of demographic change over the last century has been the dramatic increase in life expectancy. Currently, one third of the population of Europe is over 50 years old. For the financial industry, the result has been that the pension industry in particular is looking for more return on the capital it has under management.

With people generally living longer on less capital, actuaries within pension fund groups need to find routes for greater returns on money under management and many are more prepared to look at derivatives than they have been in the past. While many actuaries or pension consultants may consider looking towards derivatives for added returns the last action of desperate men, they are at least looking—which is a vast step forward.

For any manager of institutional money who is looking at either putting money into managed futures programmes, or at setting up a managed futures product for his company's investors, one of the biggest problems is finding suitable traders and having found them, then evaluating their track records.

One of the principal problems with the managed futures industry, and one that reflects its immaturity, is the lack of standardisation of reporting requirements for CTAs. This makes the job of evaluating traders' performances, and picking out the good traders from the bad, even more difficult. This subject is dealt with more fully in the next chapter. This chapter is designed to help the investor new to the field to start the evaluation process.

Here are some simple pointers to bear in mind when attempting to evaluate CTAs:

THINGS TO LOOK FOR IN EVALUATING EXISTING CTAS

- Duration of track record—what time period does the track record represent? Check that it hasn't been backdated to produce what is actually a simulated track record.
- Is the track record audited, and if so, by whom? Does the auditor have a good knowledge of the derivatives markets? It is possible to blind an accountant with science in this industry? When are profits and losses realised? How often are the accountants, or at least a third party, preparing the accounts?
- Is the CTA showing the track records of all his trades? A potential institutional investor needs to see the good, the bad and the ugly in a CTA's trading history. Check the CTA's brokers' statements.
- Is the performance of the trader consistent with his or her's methodology and market conditions. For instance, if the trader claims to be a trend-follower, how has he or she performed during a period when the markets were trending very strongly? It can also be useful to compare traders with their peers.
- Infrastructure—does the trader have the administrative back-up and experience to cope with the size of money under management that he or she already has and that which he or she may have after new investment? For some investors, particularly those that are from a pension fund background, the 'after-sales service' may be equally as important as the trader's investment performance because of fiduciary responsibilities for the money.
- Regulation—how is the trader regulated and is it to an appropriate level, given his or her geographical location? Does the trader belong to, or take an active role in, any trade associations?
- Are the trader's achievements dependent on the amount of money under management? Some traders have systems that cannot cope with trading a lot of money. Industry experts estimate that from US$ 5m to US$ 80m under management, traders run a big risk of 'blowing up' and losing performance. One way of limiting the chance of this happening in a trader to whom an investor gives money is to look at . . .
- . . . Pedigree—this is probably the most important factor to take into consideration when evaluating existing CTAs. Does the CTA have a background where he or she is used to trading money and particularly used to trading a large amount of money? A phenomenon of the European emerging CTA community is that most have an institutional background—in fact most come out of the banks. These traders are used to trading larger amounts of money and are more professional in their approach to matters such as administration and record keeping.

Beyond these points, methods such as calling for spot audits on a trader's performance record and the completion of due diligence tests should help in compiling a profile. However, evaluating new and rising traders is a more difficult proposition altogether.

EVALUATING NEW TRADERS

While many of the above points are still pertinent in looking at new traders, the most fundamental point may be that their existing track record is inextricably wound up with that of the institution for which they have been working. In this case, a qualitative evaluation becomes more important, and the following points may help.

Things to look for in evaluating new traders:

- Does the trader's work experience include trading for an institution and if so, how long has the trader been working in that institution? Ideally this should be a period of at least two years.
- Does the trader's system of trading rely on analysis or is he or she effectively a 'flow trader' making investment decisions on the basis of observation rather than analysis of those observations?
- Does the character of the trader's programme suit his or her own character? Is it plausible that this trader is able to trade in this way?
- Is the trader's experience very local, or would it stretch to other markets?
- Is the trader's programme robust?
- Does the CTA think in terms of a percentage return on equity rather than a total dollar return to the client? It is essential that the potential CTA has a firm understanding of the importance of the bigger picture when handling client money, rather than just chasing after the last drop of performance.

SOURCES OF HELP

Trading Managers

If the process of choosing CTAs oneself appears simply too onerous, there are other options. In an effort to combat the particular problem of picking good from bad, some members of the managed futures industry recommend that an institution approaching this market employs the services of a trading manager. This is someone who works on behalf of the institutional investor, selecting trading advisers or CTAs to invest the money, and monitoring their performance once chosen.

Typically, trading managers are independent. Some trading managers manage only their own CTAs, most often because they have themselves developed from a CTA background, while others can act independently of in-house CTAs and choose any trader whose performance fits into the risk/reward profile of the fund.

While trading managers can certainly be an enormous help for the institutional fund manager new to the managed futures sector, the one big problem with using them is that they usually bring with them a new layer of fees with which to burden a fund. Given that the fashion is now for funds with lower fee structures, a trading manager may inhibit that objective. However, it is equally fair to say that trading managers are the subject of much closer scrutiny than has been seen before. In the role of an interface between the trading advisers and clients, the trading manager may, in fact, achieve significant cuts on fees.

Pension Consultants

Certainly in the UK, most pension funds employ consultancy firms who provide advanced actuarial and research services to support any changes or developments in their investment policies. Most of these firms have some knowledge of derivatives, although it can remain fairly hidden within the group. It may well be worth the while of a potential investor to hunt out the derivatives expert.

GOING IT ALONE

The final option for the determined professional investor considering making an investment in managed futures is to do it alone. This is a trend that is particularly visible in Europe. It has several major advantages over using outside consultants.

Taking a serious look at the managed futures markets, doing the research and following the learning curve is firstly cheaper than using outside help and secondly can lead to greater confidence in making decisions.

In trying to find and evaluate suitable CTAs independently, the first thing, as always, is to do an extensive amount of homework. Researching the subject, by reading books such as this one, is an invaluable way to put down a fundamental knowledge for the next stage of the learning curve.

Assessing Requirements

A potential investor in any financial sector needs to analyse and define his or her requirements from that sector. In this case, the investor needs to particularly concentrate on what risk profile the funds going into a managed futures programme can endure.

Risk profiles vary considerably. If the money that is going into a managed futures programme is effectively money that can afford to be lost — in the worst case scenario — then clearly the requirement is for a trader who has a roller-coaster track record with 300 per cent gearing and massive volatility.

If however, the money going into the managed futures programme is pension fund money which carries with it a need to satisfy the requirements of its trustees that it is the sensible investment of a prudent man, then the ideal type of trader of a managed futures programme will be one who has very limited drawdowns (negative performance), steady positive returns and can prove both those things over a decent length of time.

Track Records

It will not come as much of a surprise to learn that most traders claim to have marvellous track records. In checking whether a trader is giving an accurate representation of his performance, the investor can use one of the evaluating services mentioned in the next chapter. These types of companies carry historical and current data on CTA performance which can give the investor a profile of the sort of trader under consideration.

Capital Adequacy

Despite the fact that CTAs don't actually handle client money, they merely advise on the trading of it, it appears that European CTAs may fall under the requirements of the EC's Capital Adequacy Directive (CAD). At the time of writing, the situation is not terribly clear.

European CTAs may be forced to maintain up to Ecu 730 000 (US$ 875 000) in capital reserves in order to meet the requirements of the CAD, according to various interpretations. There are three brackets of initial capital requirements for investment firms under the directive, but it appears increasingly likely that CTAs will fall into the highest category.

At the same time as the CAD announcement, the UK's Securities and Futures Authority announced the recognition of a new regulatory classification DFM, derivatives fund manager, with a capital adequacy requirement of only £10 000 (US$ 15 000). This formal recognition of CTAs as a distinct category of SFA members was secured only after a year-long campaign and protracted negotiations at a working party made up of CTAs and SFA enforcement officers. With the CAD announcement it appears that these provisions will be over-ridden when the directive comes into force on 1 January 1996.

Lobbying is being conducted at domestic UK and European level by the industry and the SFA. It may prove to be the case that those CTAs who trade proprietary money to establish a performance record will almost certainly push CTAs into the highest bracket, making it extremely difficult for emerging traders to establish themselves.

7
Performance Measurement

For an industry that prides itself — and indeed sells itself — on its performance, there is surprisingly little consistency on how to measure that performance. However, accurate performance measurement will be essential for any institution which is thinking of:

- investing in a managed futures fund or pool;
- establishing a managed futures fund and choosing CTAs to invest the money in that fund.

EXISTING SOURCES OF INFORMATION ON PERFORMANCE

There are currently various proprietary measurement systems available to investors in managed futures which measure either the performance of funds or the performance of CTAs.

The oldest, and therefore the most comprehensive in terms of historic data, of the existing measurement services is probably the various systems run by Managed Account Reports (Mar), which has performance measurement for both funds and CTAs. Mar also has five indexes: the CTA Equal-Weighted Index; the CTA Dollar-Weighted Index; the European Trading Adviser Index; the Futures Fund Index; and the Futures Pool Index.

Other Relevant Indexes

Managed funds: Barclay CTA Index; Ferrell FX Index; Norwood Futures Index; TASS CTA Equity-weighted Index.

Commodity market indexes: Commodity Research Bureau Index (CRB Index); Goldman Sachs Commodity Index (GSCI); Mount Lucas Management Index (MLM Index).

The Barra/MLM Index: this index was first produced by the Mount Lucas Group in 1988 and was designed to represent the levels of risk and return available to futures fund managers, and act as a benchmark of futures industry performance for pension funds.

The index has subsequently been studied and expanded on in a joint venture between MLM and Barra, the Californian based firm of quantitative analysts. The index uses a simple 12 month moving average trend following algorithm to track the risk/return profile of investment in the USA's 25 most liquid exchange traded contracts. There is now a fund whose investment policy is based on the index.

Other Sources

TASS Management in London is an electronic database which tracks the performance of futures investment managers worldwide, both of CTAs and futures funds.

Managed Derivatives magazine is published out of London and carries statistics and analysis on futures funds worldwide on a monthly and quarterly basis. Contact details are given on page 176 below.

PERFORMANCE MEASUREMENT—THE ISSUES

The purpose of performance measurement in managed futures is quite clear. It is to establish from a statistical perspective how 'good', 'bad' or 'indifferent' the performance is of a particular trading adviser.

All performance analysis is a study of the historical track record and there can be no guarantee that whatever has been achieved in the past can be achieved again in the future. Gaining historical information itself is difficult in this industry because of its short history.

The objective of analysis is simply to get an indication of the likelihood and capability of an adviser of managing risk and generating returns. Performance measurement is usually based on a review of returns over the monthly, quarterly, semi-annual and annual figures. For more detailed study, there could also be an analysis of daily returns.

A word of caution: The results of analysis are dependent on the accuracy and quality of the performance figures, when proffered by the performer, as well as the measures used. This should be the easiest of the performance measurer's problems to face but, inevitably, the quality of performance figures varies considerably.

Unresolved Issues in Measuring CTA Performance

The following is a list of unresolved issues connected with performance measurement for CTAs or managed futures funds. The questions raised should help an institutional investor approaching this market for the first time to focus on potential problems.

CTAs in the US who are registered as traders have to prepare their tables in a quasi 'standard format' laid down by the CFTC. No such requirement exists for CTAs based in other parts of the world, including Europe, although EMFA, the European Managed Futures Association, is planning to address this problem. Until it does, the CFTC can register the performance of non-US CTAs. Many European CTAs take this route simply in order to gain that level of recognition of their performance and to attract the attention of US investors.

However, despite the semblance of order in the US, there are still some problems because not all traders conform to exactly the same column format in presenting their returns.

Interest Income

Meaden from TASS Management says:

> Some include interest income in their performance results—others do not. All the money not used for either initial or variation margin will be sitting on deposit somewhere in T-Bills or some other short-term instruments. Some of those who include interest income in their results, charge management and/or performance fees on the interest earned. Others exclude interest income from the fees charged and only charge on the actual trading results.
>
> Some traders report only in the six or seven column format, but actually include interest income which you do not see. Anyone analysing a number of track records should make sure that they know whether or not interest income is included.

Additions and Redemptions

Another problem for the potential performance measurer is the treatment of capital additions and/or withdrawals on a monthly basis. The CFTC regulations now include a further requirement that traders should time-weight the additions and withdrawals. Meaden says:

> If a trading adviser starts off with US$ 25m under management at the beginning of the month and receives an addition of US$ 10m during the course of the month, how and when should this US$ 10m be accounted for? Depending upon whether it is accounted for at the beginning or end of the month, or on a time-weighted basis throughout the month, the final monthly percentage rate of return figure will vary. The CFTC requires time weighting, but it is possible to use a number of accepted formulae.

Fee-charging

The timing of fee-charging also presents difficulties. CTAs charge fees at different times. Incentive fees are usually charged quarterly in arrears. However, some CTAs charge management fees quarterly in advance and incentive fees quarterly in arrears. Others charge management fees quarterly in arrears, but accrue these fees on a monthly basis. Some charge management fees either monthly in advance or in arrears. There are no fixed rules on when exactly fees should be charged. The ideal solution is to strip out all fees to level the funds.

Gearing

The level of gearing in a fund is also a difficult thing to measure. Does the trading adviser's record include accounts at different levels of gearing (for example, fully funded accounts versus accounts which are funded with notional equity)? If it does, is it important or is it more accurate to look only at the fully funded accounts? The regulators take this view, but the traders generally regard their tables, which include notional equity, as more representative of their performance.

Actual or simulated trading?

Does the performance by the CTA represent actual trading for client accounts? In recent years, some CTAs have extracted all the currency trades from a diversified portfolio and presented this currency 'record' as a separate currency trading program. The CTA should only present this as a separate table once he has solicited separate business to be managed specifically in the currency program.

COMMON PERFORMANCE MEASUREMENT TOOLS AND PHRASES

- *Percentage rate of return:* Usually the average compound of the gain or loss on an investment during a specified period of time.
- *Worst ever drawdown:* A drawdown in managed futures jargon is quite simply a loss. This type of drawdown is the worst peak to valley loss, relative to the peak. It is usually calculated using monthly data.
- *Standard deviation*: This is a measure of the volatility of returns. The lower the number, the better it is if you want low historic volatility. Standard deviation is technically defined as the square root of the average of the squared deviations of monthly rates of return from the arithmetic-mean rate of return: the standard deviation measures the average spread of monthly returns around the mean.
- *Semi-deviation:* This is a measure of downside risk. It is calculated in the same way as standard deviation except that it only looks for the

observations that fall below the mean. Standard deviation only tells you how volatile the historic record has been. What it does not tell you is whether this volatility has been on the positive or the negative side. The semi-deviation figure will tell you this. So, if the semi-deviation figure is lower than the standard deviation figure then the historic volatility has been more on the upside. If the semi-deviation figure is higher than the standard deviation figure, then in the past the volatility has been more on the downside. What it does not do, of course, is tell you whether or not this pattern will continue.

- *Sharpe ratio:* This is a measure of risk/reward. This ratio tries to quantify the relationship between reward and risk by removing the risk-free rate of return. There are a number of ways to calculate Sharpe ratio. One of them is to take the average monthly rate of return, subtract from this the risk-free rate of return (for example, the return that could have been achieved if the money allocated to investment in futures was instead allocated to investment in relatively risk-free instruments such as US treasury bills) and divide this by the standard deviation of the monthly rates of return. What you are left with is the reward for pure risk-taking. The higher the ratio, the better the performance and vice versa.

  Meaden comments that there are two main weaknesses to using Sharpe ratio as a measure of risk:

  > First, it is essential to have faith in all components of the equation. Secondly, there are a number of different methods which can be used to compute the ratio. If you are comparing different Sharpe ratios, make sure that they have been computed using the same formula.

- *Risk of ruin:* The chance the investor has of losing the lot or, as Baratz rather more elegantly puts it: 'The probability that an account's original value will be reduced by a predetermined percentage as a result of trading losses.'

Common Terms Used in Measurement of Futures Funds

- *Sponsor:* the company or individual responsible for launching the fund for example, for a limited partnership, the sponsor is the General Partner
- *Trading manager or pool operator:* this is the company or individual responsible for the development of the fund both initially and on an ongoing basis
- *Domicile:* the legal home of the fund
- *Clearing broker:* the main clearing broker for the fund. Some funds use more than one broker; in such a case, the entry will read 'various'
- *Current traders:* those most recently advised by the fund manager

In 1993, the Managed Futures Association published a study on performance measurement, *Performance Measurement — Views on evaluating the returns of managed futures investments* which contained the opinions of some 21 members of the Association. Here are some of the conclusions that these practitioners in the managed futures industry reached on the statistical background to performance measurement and the problems of the lack of a common set of accounting principles.

Peter Matthews, partner and chief portfolio strategist with Mint Investment Management Company, took on the statistical view of measurement of performance. He pointed out that the basic constituents of a CTA's track record are a variety of accounts managed for different clients. The CTA's performance is a composite of these accounts. He says:

> If you are investing in a company like IBM it may not matter; since you are buying the whole company you don't particularly care how each division is doing or whether results vary a lot from one division to another. In the case of selecting a CTA, however, you are not "buying" the CTA.

What the prospective investor should do, according to Matthews, is look for the variability between the client accounts under his management:

> If the CTA achieved essentially the same return within each month for each of the clients under his management, then the composite result is representative of the CTA's performance and is a useful guide to the potential client. Conversely, if the results from one account to another in the same month are highly variable, the summary numbers are not informative.

Matthews then goes on to argue that CTA historical performance figures do not represent the outcome of a fixed statistical process and so the usual statistical inference procedures are not suitable for use. He finally concludes that because of this 'it is unrealistic to believe that one can develop "optimum" CTA portfolios on statistical grounds.'

Just in case the picture Matthews is painting for statisticians looking at this market is not gloomy enough, he finds further that there is no correlation between the historic and future returns of advisers. Referring to a recent study conducted by Scott Irwin of Ohio State University, Matthews says:

> Past returns of advisors (generally multi-advisor groups) prior to their inclusion in public futures funds have no correlation with future returns. In fact, the actual returns after the fund started have been much lower than the historical returns. The best estimate of the futures returns is the historical prior average of all public funds, not the historical returns of the CTAs selected. This is clear evidence of the difficulty of projecting future performance from historical performance.

Another interesting study which arises from the MFA's report is the examination of whether traders are skilful or lucky. Douglas G Mitchell, PhD, from CCA Capital Management took this subject on. He reports that luck can play a major role over the short term (a few years) for the futures trader but skill is the fairly permanent ability to consistently make profits from futures trading. As Mitchell says: 'An advisor cannot be lucky forever'.

The Successful Discretionary Override

Mitchell cites a series of examples to support his views:

1983 was a very difficult year for most traders. One trader had an outstanding year mainly because he sold soya beans short, right at the top of a big bull market. He made huge profits in the subsequent price decline. His 50 per cent year was the result, not of his skill per se, but of one event — having picked the top of a major bull market. He never repeated this first-class performance and subsequently faded away.

Favourable Market Selection

A trend-following trading advisor aggressively trades the 10 year Japanese bond. Our studies of this market show that for the last five years, it has been very easy to trade using trend-following techniques. So easy, in fact, that large profits have been virtually unavoidable. I estimate that trading this market has added something on the order of 15 to 20 per cent per year to the advisor's performance. The decision to aggressively trade this market was made several years ago, with little information to support it. This has been a successful decision, but probably with more luck than skill.

The Stop that Just Happened to be Right for a Major Event

European currencies, and particularly the D-mark, sold off sharply during the Russian coup attempt in August 1991. Most systematic traders were stopped out of their long positions and many reversed to being short. The coup failed and the currency markets rapidly recovered. Most systematic traders had major losses. A few lucky traders had stops in just the right place and stayed long. This was the winning strategy this time. (Had the coup succeeded, the currency collapse would probably have continued and reversed the above outcome.)

Lucky Decisions Made for Non-investment Reasons

A discretionary trader may take a vacation and miss some very good or very bad markets. A trader may have decided to trade foreign interest rate markets, just before the huge price moves we have had over the last few years.

The Small Trader Effect

A trader may be successful mainly because he uses strategies which are not viable with larger amounts of equity. His track record could be based on thinly traded options and futures markets. Future investors may not be so lucky.

The Key Event Effect

There may be very few events which affect trading performance; the fewer the events, the easier it is to be lucky or unlucky. The stock-market is a good example. A "buy and hold" trader in US stocks only needed to have predicted the 1982 bottom and the 1987 peak to generate an outstanding 12 year track record.

The Lottery Effect—Someone Has to Win

Each year the managed futures industry attracts huge numbers of aspiring but unknown traders. Those with good performance report their data to the public. The failures are never seen. This sets up conditions where investors can easily mistake good luck for superior skill.

To illustrate, suppose 4000 aspirants begin trading funds this year, and market conditions are fairly difficult. We can reasonably expect, say, 5 per cent of these to have at least minimal trading skills and enough good luck to produce attractive performance. By the end of the first year, we will have 200 apparent stars, and a few genuine ones. The remaining 3800 traders will have failed. After another fairly difficult year, given our probability factor of 5 per cent, we can expect a group of 10 to have continued good luck and good performance. Thus, two years of "stellar" performance can easily be due to luck.

In the third year, another phenomenon might occur—good luck for a whole group. Markets could be so favourable for certain trading styles that good performance almost cannot be avoided. For example, trend-followers almost couldn't fail to be very profitable in 1987, or in the late 1970s and early 1980s. Thus, it is quite possible for traders with minimal skills to generate excellent multi-year track records.

Mitchell is certain that good performance over the longer term is the only way to tell luck from skill, but if that type of data is not available, he has the following suggestions for evaluating shorter trader history:

- Using qualitative information to eliminate some lucky traders.
- Excluding all biased data including simulated track records and extracted trades.
- Basing the evaluation on a statistically significant number of events, rather than a statistically significant number of trades.

Writing in the same MFA study, Arthur Bell, partner in Arthur Bell Jr & Associates, which specialises in accounting and auditing for the managed futures industry in the US, looked at accounting standards for the managed futures industry. The subject has not been studied in any depth out of the US and the added fact that most non-US CTAs are looking to raise money in the US and so need to fit the American guidelines, means that the US experience is universally relevant.

Bell states that:

> Performance results are meaningful only when a universal reference, standard or procedure exists to quantify and measure financial activity.

The standards that currently apply to performance measurement in this industry are the usual ones: the Generally Accepted Accounting Principles (GAAP), the Regulatory Accounting Procedures (RAP) and the Private Accounting Procedures (PAP). All of these are set against the consequence of having no accounting standards, which Bell calls: Zero Accounting Procedures (ZAP).

GAAP will be familiar to most readers. It is the basic set of accounting principles which is applied to all financial statements produced both within and outside the USA, and it was set up by the Financial Accounting Standards Board (FASB). Independent auditors are required to state any exceptions or departures from GAAP which have a material effect on the fairness of the financial statements in question.

RAP is set out under the Commodity Exchange Act, the Securities Acts and the Regulations and Rulings issued by the CFTC and the SEC.

Beyond these accounting principles are those set by private sector organisations, such as in the report published by Liffe, summarised in this chapter.

As a result of the sheer number of organisations of all types working on performance reporting and accountancy and auditing issues in the managed futures industry, Bell finds that some 'vacuum areas' still exist.

> As the complexity of existing performance reporting standards increases, so does the potential for misapplication of such standards. For example, if a trading advisor realized 5 per cent on an account open for only one day of a month, reporting a time-weighted rate of return of 150 per cent would be a clear misapplication of existing standards, even if technically in conformity with the standards.

Further, he estimates that there are some six alternative methods for calculating and/or presenting the rate of return applicable to performance for a given period.

In conclusion, Bell calls for the managed futures industry to set up its own industry-wide standards-setting group to make recommendations to reduce alternative presentations of similar data, improve informative disclosure, deal promptly with emerging issues of the industry and represent the industry's interest at the various other standard-setting institutions.

THE REPORTING AND PERFORMANCE MEASUREMENT OF FINANCIAL FUTURES AND OPTIONS IN INVESTMENT PORTFOLIOS IN THE UK

One of the many obstacles placed in the way of institutions in Europe that are keen to use futures and options in their institutional portfolios has been that the trustees responsible for those portfolios would not know how to fulfil their responsibilities in those funds and that performance measurement of such portfolios would be extremely difficult.

In an effort to combat this problem in the UK at least, Liffe and LTOM (the London Traded Options Market, which is now part of Liffe) published their final recommendations for the reporting and performance measurement of financial futures and options in investment portfolios, early in 1992.

These recommendations aimed to lay down a standard for the treatment of futures and options which:

- can be adopted by all parties in the investment industry; and
- demonstrates to pension fund trustees the effect of futures and options on their portfolio performance simply and without further complicating portfolio variations.

The recommendations have been endorsed by the Investment Committee of the National Association of Pension Funds (NAPF) and the two largest independent performance measurement organisations in the UK—Combined Actuarial Performance Services (CAPS) and the World Markets Company (WM). The report was written by Mercer Fraser's Asset Planning Services department with further consultancy from Bacon & Woodrow.

A full copy of the report is available from Liffe—contact Rachel Clarke on 071 623 0444.

The following is a summary of the recommendations. While currently only applicable in the UK, these recommendations are the most developed in the European market and could indicate how institutions in other countries may treat futures and options once the regulatory path is open to them.

The scope of the Liffe report for trustees was that the recommendations were directed towards the use of futures and options contracts for portfolio management purposes as a means of gaining, reducing or modifying exposure to the asset or asset class underlying the contract. Consequently, they are not intended for application to the use of futures and options as a separate investment class in their own right.

The report specifically states:

> Different treatment should be considered for the reporting and measurement of specialist futures and options funds.

The general principles listed in Liffe's report, which apply equally to futures and options, are:

(i)   Futures and options positions should be individually listed in an intelligible way within the portfolio valuation directly under other holdings in the relevant asset (or asset class).
(ii) This listing should value the positions at their market value.
(iii) Additional material may be required as part of the portfolio valuation to ensure that the fund's true exposure is properly understood.

Individual Treatment of Futures

Reporting

The general principle is that where the exposure of the portfolio to different asset classes has been changed through the use of futures, this should be both recognised and explicit. Thus in the reporting process, the true level of exposure, the associated economic exposure, should be shown.

A futures contract represents a transaction with delayed settlement. Thus a long futures position is equivalent to purchasing the underlying asset with delayed or borrowed payment. Therefore a long FT-SE 100 futures position together with a holding in cash creates an asset which behaves like the FT-SE 100 index. An explicit adjustment should be shown in the portfolio valuation to recognise this.

In this case, the adjustment is made by increasing the UK equity exposure and reducing the cash exposure of the portfolio by the associated economic exposure of the futures position. Similarly, a short futures position is equivalent to selling the underlying asset with delayed receipt. So holding the stocks comprising the FT-SE 100 index together with a short FT-SE 100 futures position creates an asset which behaves like cash.

Here the adjustment required is to reduce the UK equity exposure and increase the cash exposure of the portfolio, again by the associated economic exposure of the futures position.

Where there is insufficient cash to back a long futures position, the portfolio has geared its exposure to the underlying assets. The same reporting procedure must be followed in such cases. This will show that the cash position is effectively overdrawn, making the nature of the gearing clear to the reader.

Associated economic exposure is, in all cases, calculated by reference to the market price of the futures contract.

Performance Measurement

The true asset allocation of the portfolio, including the associated economic exposure of the futures position, should be used in the measurement calculations.

It is necessary therefore to adjust the components of return within individual asset classes to reflect this modified exposure.

It is thoroughly recommended that the capital gain on the futures contracts should be allocated to the underlying asset class. Interest earned on the cash backing the futures should be transferred between the cash sector and the underlying asset class. For a long futures position, interest would be transferred from the cash sector to the underlying asset class. For a short futures position, the transfer would be from the underlying asset class to the cash sector.

Individual Treatment of Options

Reporting

Options contracts can be used for a wide variety of strategies, and the behaviour of the contracts themselves will not be the same for positive and negative price movements. It is, therefore, not possible to produce a single statement of exposure which accurately reflects the true position of the portfolio.

In accordance with the recommendations made by the Stonefrost Committee for Performance Measurement commissioned by the NAPF, we favour a relatively simple treatment. The central summary of the portfolio should value any options positions at their market value.

However, because this is not fully informative it should be supplemented in two ways:

1. Written explanation of the strategies being employed should be given.
2. Where the use of options is material there should be a subsidiary analysis showing the sensitivity of the options and the asset underlying the option to market movements. The depth of this analysis should reflect the specific needs of the audience to whom the report is addressed.

For externally managed funds, such as pension funds, the only requirement is that the sensitivity of the portfolio to a large positive and a large negative market movement be shown. This could be supplemented with intermediate reports if either the managers or their trustees wish to do so. On the other hand, internally managed funds with different risk profiles can adopt more complex and wide-ranging formats if they wish.

It has been necessary to develop a test to establish whether the use of options is material. This is done by assessing the size of all options positions, irrespective of whether they are long or short, against the total portfolio. Where this ratio exceeds a certain amount, the supplementary reporting process outlined above is triggered.

Performance Measurement

Option positions are valued at market value and so the capital gain or loss on the options positions would therefore be credited to the underlying asset class.

8
Marketing Issues

The author would like to thank Simon Rostron from Rostron Parry for his help with this chapter.

SOME GENERALISATIONS

The regulations currently concerning the registration, promotion and sale of derivatives funds in Europe are covered in Part Two of this book. While these regulations are complex, or alternatively, ill-defined, two generalisations are possible.

The first is that European citizens may buy derivatives funds wherever these funds are registered and in whatever form they take. The second is that it is normally possible to promote derivatives funds to residents of a European country who are not its citizens and who do not naturally speak its language—in other words to the expatriate community of a country—at least as a first option.

Both generalisations require definition. The first, the freedom to purchase, is a European feature, given for virtually all classes of investment, and is in almost diametrical opposition to the regulatory system that exists in the US. Whereas in Europe, particularly in countries such as the UK and Germany, the principal concern of the promoter or salesman is the method by which the derivatives fund is marketed to the potential purchaser, in the US or, more accurately, when dealing with US citizens, it is inevitably illegal to allow the purchase of an unapproved fund.

The second generalisation is more important for marketeers of offshore funds seeking to sell their products in Europe than for the increasing number of funds registered within one European jurisdiction.

Let us take two examples, one inside and one outside the European Community. In Switzerland, it is usually dangerous, from a regulatory standpoint, to attempt to promote a fund through press relations (a common method in the majority of other countries), particularly when the contact between marketeer and journalist takes place in Switzerland and is intended to result in coverage in a newspaper or magazine published within the country in one of the four official languages (German, French, Italian and Romanisch).

It is not, however, a problem to use press relations to promote a fund to Swiss residents when the press coverage appears, say, in an English language publication whose circulation is not focused on Switzerland (such as the *International Herald Tribune, The Economist, Financial Times, Managed Derivatives* and so on).

An equivalent position occurs in Spain particularly with regard to the expatriate community, which is concentrated along the country's southern coastline. This community has its own publications and is also one of the targets of a series of expatriate and offshore magazines, largely devoted to financial matters and usually produced in the UK. This reflects the fact that most of the expatriates concerned are British.

Within these two groups of publications it is possible to promote derivatives funds not registered in Spain or other EC member states. This promotion can be done using press relations and, often, advertising routes. Furthermore, Gibraltar television, received by residents of Spain and Portugal within a radius of at least one hundred miles from the Rock, could be used as a promotional vehicle.

It is fair to add here that Spanish publications, particularly those serving the financial community, increasingly discuss managed derivatives funds whether registered in the country or not but they may not be used to promote such products in a more direct sense.

The two examples above largely focus on press relations which has historically been and continues to be one of the prime methods conveying information about managed derivatives funds. The examples also specifically relate to the retail marketing of funds unapproved in a particular country—the activity upon which the majority of national regulators are focused. Marketing to institutions in Europe can be characterised by another generalisation: it is generally permissible to promote managed derivatives funds, derivatives managers and derivatives management programmes to institutions provided that the methods used do not also impact in any significant way (that breaches regulations) on actual or potential retail investors.

MARKETING OBJECTIVES

Within the context of the managed futures industry in Europe, there are, loosely divided, six marketing objectives depending on the product being offered and the type of company or group which is offering it. These are:

- sales of funds or management programmes to investment institutions;
- CTAs attempting to manage money within (usually) multi-manager funds or equivalent investment products;
- sales by fund management groups, to expatriate retail investors or, increasingly (with domestically registered funds) to retail investors within their own countries;
- fund management groups seeking joint venture partners for the creation and distribution of funds (usually retail) within an individual country or economic block;
- fund management groups seeking sales agents to distribute products on a commission basis in a defined area;
- consultancy groups attempting to act for investment management groups — particularly those considering multi-manager derivatives funds, to structure the fund, select CTAs and control asset allocation.

MARKETING TECHNIQUES

Each of the above objectives implies a tailored marketing programme but before discussing the details and perceived results of the various techniques, one further generalisation is possible. That is, with the exception of cold calling and product advertising (except in so far as advertising may be used to promote country registered funds within that country, and to certain groups of expatriates, and non-specific corporate advertising), all familiar methods of investment marketing may be employed.

Shot-gun Marketing Techniques

These methods include shotgun marketing techniques such as:

- press relations;
- mailings to institutions;
- corporate, but not specific product, advertising;
- conferences/seminars.

Rifle-shot Marketing Techniques

These methods include the more specific rifle-shot techniques such as:

- presentations (to invited groups);
- 'promo' lunches;
- one on one meetings.

Competitive Fee Structure Techniques

In addition certain fund groups build sales promotion facets within the structure of their funds or within the offer documents. These elements can include:

- Sales fees declining in inverse proportion to the capital invested—the more the investor puts into a fund, the less it will cost.
- Discounted share prices during the offer period (for open-ended funds).

Fund management groups which have employed these techniques report that they are equally as likely to appeal to institutional as well as to retail investors—a discounted entry price (particularly if accompanied by a competitive overall fee structure) tends to overcome one of the principal sticking points to European institution investment—high costs.

Relating Familiar Marketing Techniques to Managed Derivatives Targets

European Institutions

The preparedness of European institutions to purchase either managed derivatives funds or programmes varies across the continent and is dependent upon a series of factors some of which may be addressed by marketing.

- The regulatory (and tax) environment;
- general familiarity with the derivatives and managed derivatives industry;
- familiarity with the fund management group attempting to sell product;
- presence and format of a track record (at least for past funds if a new product is offered);
- money under management within the fund group;
- technical expertise within the fund group;
- performance aspirations for the fund or investment programme;
- quality and content of the explanatory/sales materials;
- financial considerations such as fees implicit within the fund or programme.

Regulatory and Tax Environment

Clearly, marketing techniques (except political lobbying which is almost inevitably the function, in Europe, of trade associations) can have little impact on the regulatory and tax environment whose absence of clarity in certain European countries inhibits institutional enthusiasm for managed derivatives products.

That said, experiences cited by fund managers prove that it is a serious marketing error to make general assumptions based on perceived regulatory problems within a country or financial centre and on a negative reception from the first batch of institutions contacted.

Indeed, at least one major fund group preferentially employs salesmen without significant derivatives experience to overcome preconceptions about the impossibility of sales to certain types of institutions or within certain geographical areas — with very successful results.

It is, however, possible to make assumptions about better and worse institutional prospects particularly in the context of more or less receptive countries or financial centres. In broad terms centres with derivatives exchanges include banks and other financial institutions familiar, to some degree, with the derivatives business. This can be because either at worst the exchange generates press coverage or at best because the institution in question is a trading member.

This is not to say that the gap between derivatives understanding and managed derivatives investment is narrow but it does serve to enable fund management companies and others contemplating a marketing/sales campaign to make some choices about suitable areas on which to focus.

Increasing Familiarity — Press Relations

Embarking on a marketing effort with the major European financial centres as the initial focus is, however, extremely arduous for new, particularly non-European, groups.

Given appropriate lists of contacts, one-on-one meetings can be arranged relatively straightforwardly, but their effectiveness is dependent on a series of criteria beyond the chemistry of the meeting itself.

Press relations, actively undertaken, will serve both to boost familiarity of a fund management group and, moreover, can prove a valuable information source to the group as well as from it.

Over the past few years, the European press has increasingly reacted positively — with certain exceptions — to the derivatives industry as a whole and to managed derivatives in particular. Within the major financial press, for example, there are often journalists focusing on the managed derivatives sector, or who, at least, include that sector within their overall 'beat'. Furthermore, financial or investment trade magazines are continuing to expand their coverage and, in countries such as France, Germany and the UK, trade magazines have been launched with derivatives or managed derivatives as a specific focus.

Major derivatives groups or major name investment groups (or banks) entering the managed derivatives sector have little difficulty obtaining useful press coverage which (copyright notwithstanding) they often reprint to use as an additional marketing tool. But this coverage inevitably arises from a close relationship, developed over time — and lunch, in the time-honoured fashion — between the group and the publication in question.

Selection of Major European Financial Newspapers (or newspapers which include useful derivatives coverage)

Austria *Die Presse*
Belgium *De Financieel Ekonomische Tijd, L'Echo*
Denmark *Berlingske Tidende, Borsen*
Finland *Aamulehti, Kauppalehti*
France *Agefi, Figaro, Les Echos, La Tribune Desfosses, Le Monde*
Germany *Boersen Zeitung, Frankfurter Allgemeine Zeitung, Handelsblatt*
Greece *Kerdos*
Ireland *The Irish Press, The Irish Times*
Italy *Corriere della Serra, Il Sole/24 Ore*
Luxembourg *Luxemburger Wort, Tageblatt*
The Netherlands *Algemeen Dagblad, De Telegraaf, Het Financieele Dagblad, NRC Handelsblad*
Norway *Aftenposten, Norges Handels og Sjofartstidende*
Portugal *Diario Economico*
Spain *ABC, Cinco Dias, El Mundo, El Pais, La Vanguardia*
Sweden *Dagens Industri, Dagens Nyheter, Svenska Dagbladet*
Switzerland *Agefi, Corriere del Ticino, Finanz und Wirtschaft, Journal de Geneve, Neue Zurcher Zeitung*
Turkey *Hurriyet, Milliyet*
UK *Financial Times, The Independent*
International *International Herald Tribune, Wall Street Journal of Europe*

Gaining Profile—Press Relations

The development of such a relationship is dependent on taking time out to meet journalists. Normally such meetings may be arranged during the course of a trip to a particular area. Expecting a relationship to develop on the back of press releases and the occasional telephone call will not work.

Once familiarity with at least some members of the press has been established, the fund group should expect to achieve comparatively regular coverage, particularly if the announcements it makes are tailored (or appear tailored) to the country in question. The fund group should also, with a little pushing, gain the opportunity to submit placement pieces talking more generally about the managed derivatives industry and should also be included in investment survey and so on.

It is worth noting, in that context, that the separation between editorial and advertising which is a characteristic of most national newspapers does not always hold so strongly in trade magazines and therefore the occasional expenditure of corporate advertising funds can go a long way to create friends.

The principal aim of a press relations campaign is to provide independent (or apparently independent) endorsement of the importance of particular managed derivatives so that one-on-one meetings with institutions will occur that much more easily.

Track Record

Press relations cannot, however, help with one of the more vital elements of a salesman's ammunition — track record. In the past it has been true that no European institution would consider a fund group without a relatively substantial real track record. However due to increasing concerns about performance of an investment programme tending to decline over time as the space grows between the period when the trading/investment system was developed and the present, this is no longer the case.

Track records, even if largely hypothetical should, however, include an element of real trading. They should also contain as much independent verification as available (for instance, audited accounts) and, wherever possible, be quoted net of fees and expenses. Furthermore, hypothetical track records should also recognise and account for imperfect market conditions — price slippage and the like.

It is generally not necessary, unless aiming for a fund focused on one country, to requote performance in a non-dollar currency (assuming the original performance is quoted in dollars) nor is it essential to quote comparisons against local indexes (but see Performance below). That said, in the UK a very large number of institutions measure performance against the *Financial Times* Actuaries Index (FTA).

Finally, track records should not be squeezed to produce the highest possible performance. A number of fund groups have reported that European institutions are very concerned about the balance between performance and risk and tend to be suspicious of unusually high figures fearing these cannot be repeated consistently.

MONEY UNDER MANAGEMENT

In Europe, as elsewhere in the world, institutions like when possible either to deal with specialist boutique operations or with operations the same size (or at least with the same standing in their particular industry) as themselves. Thus a middle-sized fund group with, say US$ 10m or US$ 25m under management is going to find itself with a very hard sell indeed. In these circumstances it is important, from a marketing standpoint, to quote all the capital/corporate size available. Thus if the middle-sized fund group is a subsidiary of a larger brokerage or banking operation, the capital worth of the parent should be brought into play.

If no parent company exists, attention should be focused on the specialist characteristics of the fund group and its investment programmes (words like *flexibility* and *innovative* are useful here) in an attempt to portray the fund group as a niche business. (This technique is often used by consultancy groups seeking to act for investment management groups.)

Technical Expertise

As above, anything which can distinguish a fund and its programmes is desirable. This applies to high academic standing among the personnel (the 'rocket scientists') as much as it does to the claims of rigorous testing of a technical system. Sellers of funds based upon technical systems should remember that the institution is still, to a great extent, buying the people representing the system rather than, straightforwardly, access to the 'black box'. Equally sellers of funds based on fundamental trading systems should remember and have an answer to institutional concerns about the star trader being run over by a bus, for example.

In both cases, substantiated claims of testing the investment programme in every conceivable market condition are valuable.

Performance Aspirations

The expected returns on a fund, as quoted, are, of course, largely a function of the quoted track record. In that context it is worth restating that European institutions are made nervous by apparently exorbitant potential performance. A number of institutions have been quoted in the press as saying that they are disappointed that the performance expectations are always a number of percentage points higher than the real figures (often because of the imposition of a more substantial fee structure than originally envisaged).

Furthermore, potential performance need not simply be quoted as straightforward capital growth. Increasingly, successful fund groups are quoted figures in terms of percentages above a particular benchmark or index. More specifically, certain managed derivatives programmes are sold on the basis of improving overall portfolio performance by a few percentage points. Nor need performance always be considered simply from a growth standpoint. Certain new funds, particularly those partially aimed at tax exempt institutions (such as pension funds in certain countries), offer a combination of income and performance, perhaps even guaranteeing the income levels.

If the fund being offered already has an established track record then it may prove useful to quote figures or provide graphs showing the fit between real performance and programme expectations.

So-called Guaranteed Futures Funds also have their place in this equation although these are usually much more enthusiastically received at the retail end of the market.

Explanatory Materials

Conventionally, funds are promoted in Europe through a prospectus, some form of explanatory memorandum or summary and, often, a sheaf of figures to substantiate the various financial claims. (Reprinted press cuttings may also be included in the pack.)

Prospectus

US and European prospectuses tend to differ not only in content (forced on the writers by different regulatory jurisdictions) but also in lay-out and style. Whereas in the USA, prospectuses are normally economically printed in one colour only, European prospectuses which are often significantly shorter may also double as sales support documents and may thus be produced more artistically to include performance graphs and other coloured charts. European prospectuses also often have separate (card) front covers.

Whether this distinction remains is open to question. Certain fund groups selling in Europe are beginning, for reasons of cost, to adopt the US look for prospectuses and, furthermore, are beginning to include US style information. For example, until very recently, it was uncommon for European prospectuses to include calculations of the likely number of trades per $1 million per year for a fund. Without such information it is clearly impossible to make any real judgment of brokerage commission flows—information that institutions increasingly require.

Summary

Whatever the form of the prospectus, the summary document remains the most important single sales tool. Quality of design and, hopefully, a novel approach to graphics and images within the document (in other words, no traders on telephones) reflect at an important subliminal level, the care and attention spent on preparing the fund.

Furthermore, while (subject to European regulations) a prospectus may simply be printed in English, it is unsatisfactory from a diplomatic point of view (no matter how well the representatives of the European institutions speak English) not to have the summary translated.

Summary content is largely a matter of personal choice but should certainly include all the main fund points — the style of trading, the performance history of the fund group or (if new) at least the history of the traders/investment managers, performance aspirations and the technical/financial details of the fund *including* the fees to be levied upon it. It is not sensible to produce a summary that concentrates entirely on promoting the bull points of a fund leaving the buyer to wade through the prospectus in an attempt to discover the implicit costs.

Performance Information

Wads of figures may be a necessary element of a fund's sales package but they are often inelegant to present and difficult to comprehend at a preliminary meeting. On the other hand, the majority of fund groups has always been reluctant to print large numbers of figures within either the summary or prospectus for reasons both of cost and of time sensitivity — computer printed figures give the (often true) impression of being that much more immediate.

One solution to this dilemma now being attempted by some fund groups and CTAs is to computerise figures and leave them with the institution in the form of a disk. This approach has the considerable advantage (assuming computer compatibility) of allowing the institution to recalculate the figures to suit its own particular financial requirements and, in the best case, to test run the proposed investment programme within its own portfolios to make judgments about portfolio performance enhancement and risk reduction.

Developing beyond the simple computer presentation of figures, certain fund groups, particularly those with larger sales forces or a set of international representative agents, are working with what are in effect computerised summaries — presented on (colour screen) lap top computers and easily updatable via telephone links to headquarters.

Clearly the requirement to deliver performance information does not stop with the initial contact or, indeed, with the sale itself. The majority of fund groups communicate performance figures on a regular (normally monthly) basis to their investors and potential investors — usually by fax or mail. Beyond this, considerable institutional comfort may be achieved by quoting performance figures in the appropriate sections of major international newspapers such as the *Financial Times* and/or the *Wall Street Journal*. Since all figure entries in these publications look much the same there is considerable implied kudos in being next, in a listing, to one of the famous fund groups and, moreover as the number of funds quoted increases so the impression of financial power and stability strengthens.

Fees and Other Financial Considerations

In one sense, marketing cannot affect the fee structure within a fund but fees and other financial considerations are so important a consideration to the potential fund buyer that it is worth examining the marketing impact of certain fee structures before the final shape of a fund is settled.

For example, in Europe as in the USA, the trend in funds is to increase the levels of performance fees (to 20 per cent or even 25 per cent) and concomitantly reduce levels of management fees (to 4 per cent per annum or lower). Fund groups with expectations of a high volume of sales should go lower than this.

Furthermore, European institutions and more and more European retail investors are becoming increasingly suspicious of front-end sales commissions designed primarily to encourage agents. New funds are almost always prepared to pay commissions to agents but many of them bury the costs within the overall 'costs to the fund management group'. Investors are also uncomfortable with 'penalties for early redemptions' and while these are a normal feature of guaranteed funds due to the financial structure underlying the guarantee, they should be avoided wherever possible. If the fund group is seen to be taking some of the financial risk off the institution, a sale is more likely.

One fee trend which is being examined is a reduction of fees in line with higher initial investment. This is taking place not only with regard to sales commissions (as mentioned above) but also with management fees.

One final point — minimum investment. Marketing arguments are ranged on both sides of the debate about the size of a minimum investment. Clearly if a fund is highly technical and largely only comprehensible by certain types of institution (an OTC interbank interest rate fund, for example) a very high minimum entry — perhaps US$ 1m — is justified. On the other hand, institutions are rarely taken in by a fund which sets high minimum entries (US$ 100 000) on what is otherwise a retail product simply to give the impression of being tailored specifically for the institutional market. In fact a more conventional minimum of US$ 30 000 or US$ 50 000 can often prove effective both for institutions and for the (often mythical) high networth individual.

Other Marketing Targets

The preceding pages have principally focused on marketing considerations for a fund group attempting to sell product to a European institution. The majority of the elements examined are, however, equally valid when supporting other commercial objectives such as attempting to create a joint venture with an institution or embarking on a retail sales campaign. Some modifications or amendments are, however, appropriate.

CTAS

The principal marketing objective for CTAs, unless very large or very well-known, is to be included as a money manager within multi-manager funds. The most important element in the successful attainment of this objective is performance listing and it is incumbent on a CTA to spend a considerable part of the marketing effort in making sure that as many international services as possible carry his or her figures. The critical value of such services (such as Managed Account Reports, or LaPorte) is two-fold. First they are the key distributors of performance information and as such are followed by so-called 'Hot Money'. Second they provide subscribers with an easy opportunity to make comparisons between CTAs.

It is true that some CTAs have made considerable marketing mileage out of refusing to have their figures known publicly but it is also true that some others, particularly those who have withdrawn information having formerly been quoted, have opened themselves to suspicions of financial weakness or, worse, malpractice.

CTAs also benefit in terms of profile from feature articles in the press and are normally most likely to achieve these by establishing and maintaining personal contacts with derivatives trade publications. Note—it is not necessary to be big to be famous. Long-established performance track records are not essential for successful CTA marketing. There is, in fact, increasing enthusiasm among sections of the European investment community for new names with only short real track records but an innovative approach or a narrow market focus.

For CTAs without any form of prior track record services (such as Auditrack) have been created in order to enable acceptable simulations of trading over a three or six month period to be carried out. This creates, at the end of the time, at least a plausible hypothetical track record which takes into account the various market entry and execution problems a CTA may face.

As for materials, some care (and expense) should be applied to producing not simply a computer run of trading figures but also a form of brochure introducing the CTA's trading strategy. For chartists, illustrations of the system used are helpful provided they are not so definitive and detailed as to be perceived, by non-believers, as crusading rather than trading.

RETAIL SALES

Advertising

Beyond the requirement for agents (discussed below), fund groups undertaking retail sales tend to support their marketing efforts with fund advertising. Advertising regulations are both complex and highly variable between different countries but that does not mean that effective campaigns cannot be developed.

One problem to be faced here is that the most effective marketing statement — the expected performance of a new fund — is the one most difficult to get past the regulations. (Past performance is no guarantee of future results, for example.)

Fund Structure

Retail orientated managed derivatives funds may often differ from their institutional counterparts. The best example of this is in the employment of guarantees of return of capital. So-called guaranteed funds appeared in the mid-1980s and have thus far escaped the best efforts of numbers of regulators (outside the USA) to force a name change to something less overtly promotional (assured capital funds and so on).

Guarantees have their supporters and detractors but they do sell to retail investors and investors who (in most, but not all, countries) like the assurance of a guarantee when trying a new type of investment vehicle and are less swayed by comments about performance dilution than are the institutions. Furthermore, from a marketing standpoint, the presence of a guarantee or more accurately a guarantor creates the opportunity to include the name of a bank (often a major bank) as an additional sales incentive.

Marketing Materials

There is no proof of the assertion that retail investors are more swayed by brightly coloured marketing materials than are institutions. What is clear, however, is that the content of such materials should spend time introducing the concepts of derivatives and of managed derivatives at a more basic level. One worry expressed by many fund groups is the inclusion of the notorious word *commodities* within documentation about a diversified fund and various awkward attempts have been made at euphemism.

In fact it is probable that commodities — pictured rather than discussed — have a positive rather than negative sales impact since they are much more readily comprehensible than certain classes of financial instruments. When a retail investor understands that the natural way to invest in oil or (tax-free) gold is through derivatives he or she is often on the way to becoming the purchaser of a certain type of fund.

Joint Ventures

Creating joint venture arrangements between a fund group and a financial group capable of distributing product is one of the most efficient ways to obtain investment capital, but at a price. The key requirement in arranging joint ventures is not marketing but having a clear understanding of the financial structure of the proposed fund and the income consequences of various splits of the managed or sales fees or brokerage commissions.

Marketing can help initiate discussions, however. Here, a high profile in the press is desirable, particularly if supported by occasional conference platform speeches (see below). It may also be helpful for a member of the fund management team to be an active member of a derivatives or managed derivatives trade association—to give more strings to the marketing bow.

Agents

One marketing consideration that generally affects fund groups attempting international retail sales is a need for agents in various countries.

Making contact with such agents has, in the past, normally been achieved by advertising (often classified) in such publications as *The Economist* or the *International Herald Tribune* supported by editorial coverage of a fund group's ambitions in agents' trade magazines (of which there are a growing number).

There are three principal messages that need to be put across. The first, most obviously, is the size of the upfront sales commission and of the so-called 'trail' or 'trailing commission' (the ongoing income to an agent whose clients stay with the fund). Quite reasonably, fund companies have become uncomfortable with an exclusive focus on upfront commissions since certain groups found themselves being burnt by commission earning money coming into a fund and then, mysteriously, moving on somewhere else.

The second message is support. Agents increasingly respond well to formal training sessions—both about the managed derivatives market in general as well as about the specific product on offer. Supplementing such events, many fund groups also put together specific agents packages which include simplified written explanations of aspects of the derivatives industry and on the historical/academic arguments often used to promote derivatives funds—Portfolio Diversification, Futures as a Separate Asset Class, Modern Portfolio Theory and so on.

The third message is support advertising. Agents tend to feel more comfortable with a fund if they recognise that they are gaining promotional support for their work from an advertising campaign (where regulations permit). Some fund groups undertake a form of split advertising campaign which combines general and larger advertisements running in major publications with an allowance for agents to place smaller advertisements in financial trade publications of their choice.

While agents are still contacted effectively by the techniques suggested above, a new market trend—the development of agent networks (such as EIFAN, the European Independent Financial Agents Network)—has tended to make the job of fund distribution rather simpler. Such networks normally require an upfront cash payment from the fund group to support promotional activities but, in return for that payment, should become exclusive to the fund group (at least for the type of fund being offered) for the term of the contract.

Consultancy Groups

Experience seems to show that the most important marketing act for a consultancy group seeking to advise a fund management group (possibly new into the derivatives area) on fund structure, CTA selection and others, is physical presence. The opening of a representative office in a financial centre has proved on a number of occasions to be the precursor to the development of a profitable relationship.

Beyond this, consultancy groups need, normally through marketing materials, to demonstrate a highly rigorous approach to the organisation of a fund. The outpourings of huge computer systems are often brought into play in this context to demonstrate extremes of due diligence. Unfortunately, on a number of occasions such operations have fallen prey to the computer programmer's axiom—garbage in, garbage out—which has meant that more successful consultants are now not unafraid to combine objective *and* subjective criteria in their presentations.

As a rule, a high press profile does not suit a consultancy operation since it may convey the impression of non-exclusivity, a preparedness to work with competitors and so on. Conference appearances, on the other hand, are an effective marketing ploy.

Conclusion—The Conference Circuit

Managed derivatives, like all sectors of the financial industry, is well served by conferences. Unfortunately for 'marketeers', however, by far the majority of such events are attended by competitors (and regulators) rather than by potential clients.

This feature, however, does not deny the importance of events such as the Managed Account Report Conferences in Europe, the USA and Asia, the new Managed Futures Association and Managed Derivatives events or other equivalent events. While salesmen seeking to move product or consultants seeking new entrants into the managed derivatives sector may be disappointed, fund groups looking for joint venture partners and CTAs looking for inclusion within funds are well-advised to attempt to gain a speaking position.

Becoming a speaker may be a matter of invitation — probably based on one or a series of press articles building his or her profile. It can also be a matter of developing a relationship with conference organisers ('schmoozing'), many of whom are associated with trade publications with whom the intending speaker should already have contact. For a number of the larger events, put on by industry associations, membership of the association in question is an essential precursor to getting on the speaker list.

In pushing his or her desire to speak, the individual should have prepared a sort of speaker's c.v. which lists previous engagements, specific areas of interest and expertise (as unusual as possible) and providing a brief history of the group or company he or she represents. This can be left with conference organisers after initial contact has been made.

That said, there is an easier route. Fund groups and equivalent operations are generally able to buy access to conferences by agreeing to sponsor, say, a cocktail party, the conference banquet or whatever. The important point to understand, when travelling this route, is that payment to sponsor does not automatically guarantee the sponsor's name in lights and considerable attention should be paid to ensuring that large signs at the cocktail party (or profile activities such as a game or a clever gift) are present to get the name across.

For salesmen seeking institutional targets, small short presentations are much more effective than set piece events. The notion that representatives of institutions will not turn up at such a focused event where their competitors may also be present has been proved fallacious time and again. In fact, the principal reason why such sales presentations fail on a regular basis is that insufficient attention has been given to understanding the practical requirements — the right venue, the right time of day, the right day of the week (given government announcements, public holidays) and so on.

One final comment. Many speakers claim a virtue in spontaneity and speak more or less off-the-cuff. While this approach may indeed create a better or more vigorous presentation, it fails to create a full lasting effect. The proper marketing approach is to speak off-the-cuff, if preferred, but nonetheless to have the basic text of the speech (plus print outs of any slides used) ready for distribution.

The distribution can serve a number of purposes. First, it serves to reinforce the recollections of conference delegates (and to inform those not attending that session). Secondly, it provides verbatim material for any press covering the conference. Thirdly, distributed more broadly (perhaps in a summarised form) it can be used as a supplement to other marketing materials. Fourth, it can be used to support applications to speak at other events.

The last word is about photographs — it is essential to have a good stock not only for inclusion within the conference programme but also for enhancing potential press coverage.

9
Case Studies

The aim of this chapter is to show how all the information covered in theory in the earlier chapters works in practice by describing in detail two mythical European retail managed futures funds.

The profiles in this chapter are based on two actual European funds which were launched in 1991 and 1992 respectively. Their outlines show the reasoning behind the launch of such a fund, how each participant in the fund works, how the charging structure works and the legal structure to a fund.

The names of the funds are not mentioned due to regulatory restrictions on providing details on unregulated investment schemes to the general public.

The material for the Fund A case study is drawn from the prospectus and marketing material supplied by its CPO. This fund was chosen as a study because it has a wide range of CTAs, including some of the better known and more successful CTAs based in Europe. The process of combining types of traders within one fund is a lengthy but essential one. Clearly if a range of traders are chosen who all negatively correlate with each other, the resulting fund performance could be quite flat. The aim of a multi-adviser fund is to choose a group of advisers whose performances complement each other.

The fund chosen for Fund B case study is included because it remains one of the most successful launches in Europe. The fund has a slightly different structure from the normal, with a trading manager inserted between the CPO and the CTAs. This is not unusual for potential CPOs who are new to the business and regularly choose to defer to the specialists—often American—who act as trading managers to choose and organise the fund's CTAs. In the case of Fund B, the names and track records of the CTAs are not disclosed but the fund group concerned has provided background on why it set the fund up and why it chose its particular type of structure.

CASE STUDY FOR FUND A

Information about the Fund

Legal Structure

Fund A is an open-ended Luxembourg umbrella fund—a Sicav. It is managed by the Bermudan offices of its sponsoring bank Fund A (Bermuda) Ltd. It is an umbrella fund, which means that it has a series of sub-funds—among which the investor can switch—under the one umbrella. The fund has raised, since 1991, US$ 28m.

The sub-funds in Fund A's umbrella are the Diversified Fund, the Financial Fund and the Currency Fund.

Investment Objectives

Shares in the fund come in two forms, either as trading shares or as guaranteed shares, and in several currency classes.

The investment objective of the trading shares is to achieve superior long-term capital appreciation from trading futures. Each class of trading shares will invest in futures, and the balance of cash may be invested in money-market instruments, treasury bills or other short-dated debt instruments issued or guaranteed by sovereign borrowers or other highly rated institutions or in deposits with banks and brokers (also referred to as 'short-dated debt instruments and deposits'). An investor can choose trading shares denominated in US dollars, French francs or D-Marks.

The investment objective of the guaranteed shares is to provide more cautious investors with an opportunity for capital appreciation from trading futures while ensuring the repayment of the initial investment at the maturity date. Each class of guaranteed shares will combine:

- a portfolio of futures held by the company and the balance of cash owned by the company invested in short-dated debt instruments and deposits, *with*
- the right to a payment to be made at maturity out of the fiduciary assets, consisting of a portfolio of stripped (zero coupon) debt instruments, forming normally part of a single issue, issued or guaranteed by sovereign states (the bonds) with a maturity date on or before the maturity date of the relevant class of guaranteed shares; the bonds are held by the custodian as fiduciary for the benefit of the holders of guaranteed shares.

An investor can choose guaranteed shares denominated in US dollars or French francs. The denomination of the class of share will normally determine the currency of the bonds.

If guaranteed shares are redeemed prior to the maturity date, an investor will receive, pro rata, the current net asset value of the futures pool for that class and the market value of the relevant proportion of the bonds at the time of redemption (which is likely to be less than at the maturity date) less the following redemption charge:

Redemption made before:	*Early redemption charge*
1st anniversary of subscription	4.5%
2nd anniversary of subscription	4.0%
3rd anniversary of subscription	3.0%
4th anniversary of subscription	2.0%
5th anniversary of subscription	1.0%
6th anniversary of subscription	1.0%
7th anniversary of subscription	1.0%
Thereafter	No charge

Issue Price

Trading shares: US$ 10, FFr 50 or DM 20. Guaranteed shares: US$ 10.

Minimum Investment

Minimum investment in the trading shares is US$ 20 000, FFr 100 000 or DM 30 000. In the guaranteed shares, minimum investment is US$ 5000.

Management and Administration Fees Payable to the Manager

These are 2.5 per cent per annum for trading shares and 1.5 per cent per annum for the guaranteed shares.

In addition to these commissions and the fees payable to the trading managers, the company's expenses including the directors' fees and expenses; legal, accounting and auditing fees; promotional, printing, reporting and publishing expenses, including the cost of advertising or preparing and printing of prospectuses; explanatory memoranda, or registration statements, taxes or government charges; the costs of listing the shares on any stock exchange or regulated market; and all other operating expenses. Such expenses will be borne by the company and divided among the share classes.

All of the organisational expenses and costs incurred in the initial offer of shares (estimated at US$ 250 000) and the offering fee referred to below will be borne by the company. The organisational expenses of the share classes will be amortised over a period of five years pro rata according to the total net trading assets of the respective classes.

The manager will receive an offering fee of 2 per cent of the amount raised by the offer of the shares to meet part of the distribution costs incurred in placing the shares. Such a fee will be apportioned and amortised in the same manner as the organisational expenses of the respective share classes. Such a fee will also be charged to trading shares purchased after the close of the initial offer and amortised in a similar manner to that described above.

No other sales fee will be charged to the investor.

The organisational expenses and offering fee of new share classes offered by the company will be amortised in a similar manner.

Incentive Fees and Management Fees Payable to CTAs

CTAs will get between 20 per cent and 25 per cent of net new quarterly profits (after expenses but before performance fees) earned by the company and charged to the relevant share classes. The fixed management fees, where applicable, will range between 0 per cent and 4 per cent of the net asset value of a fund's trading assets allocated to a CTA to manage. Again, such fees will be charged to the respective share classes. Fees due to a CTA will be calculated separately on the trading assets allocated to each CTA.

Brokerage

The principal broker to the fund is Fund A Brokerage Ltd. Brokerage is charged at rates varying between US$ 7.50 and US$ 25 per lot.

Taxation

The fund operates free of Luxembourg income and capital gains taxes for Luxembourg non-residents. An annual levy of 0.06 per cent is payable on the net assets of Fund A.

Switching of Shares

Investors can switch between available funds and share classes up to four times per calendar year before incurring a charge.

Investment Policies

Fund A has three sub-funds, the Currency Fund, the Financial Fund and the Diversified Fund. All three funds use multiple trading managers. Modern portfolio theory is applied to help in the selection of these trading managers. Statistical analysis of their risk-adjusted results helps to identify those which have developed superior trading systems with disciplined money management controls. The Fund A funds seek to combine several of the most profitable trading managers using different trading styles and systems to increase portfolio and management diversification and reduce risk.

Asset Allocation

Asset allocations to trading managers will be assisted by a dynamic asset allocation model. The model is designed to analyse the results of multiple combinations of CTAs with variable asset allocations according to acceptable risk/return parameters, variance of current and historic returns and the correlation of independent results.

Results of past asset allocations are compared with the results of recent allocations and are tested for statistical significance. Such robust combinations help to enhance long-term returns and reduce volatility.

The manager may select new, or remove existing, CTAs in the funds.

The Diversified Fund

Investment Objectives

The objective of this fund is to achieve superior long-term capital appreciation through trading in the major international futures, options, spot and forward contract markets (futures) in precious and base metals, stocks and other indexes, bonds, interest rates, currencies, energy and agricultural products.

The CTAs

Futures Managers Ltd.
Capital Corp.
Asset Management
Trading Company Ltd.
Futures Ltd.
Money Management Ltd.

Futures Managers Ltd. is based in Europe. Futures Managers created a sophisticated computer research test-bed to examine a variety of trading systems across a wide range of futures contracts and over long periods of time. After exhaustive tests, three highly disciplined and automated trading systems have been developed and applied to all of the major futures markets. New markets will be added as they meet the systems's requirements. Only a very small percentage of the capital allocated to Futures Managers will generally be risked on any one trade.

Capital Corp. is a US corporation which was incorporated for the purpose of offering futures investment advisory and portfolio management services to both retail and institutional investors.

Capital Corp.'s trading approach relies primarily on technical analysis. The trading methods employed by it are based on programmes analysing a large number of interrelated mathematical and statistical formulae and techniques which are quantitative and proprietary in nature and which have been developed during the past eight years by the company's principal.

In addition to mathematical evaluations, Capital Corp. also uses 'charting' and internally generated market information to analyse market conditions and to determine optimal support and resistance levels and entry and exit points in various markets. Capital Corp. applies strict money management principles based on standard probability theory to control risk.

Asset Management is a European corporation formed for the purpose of achieving capital appreciation from managed accounts in the futures markets.

Asset Management uses a technical, computerised, trend-following model to trade the futures and options markets. It does not apply a discretionary overlay to trading decisions. Trading strategies will be enhanced or revised from time to time, although the basic principles are expected to remain substantially the same.

Asset Management will monitor and trade a diversified portfolio of over 40 US and international markets including currencies, financial instruments, the energy complex, precious and base metals and agricultural markets.

Trading Company Ltd. is a Bermudan corporation. Trading Company Ltd. relies more on technical than on fundamental analysis, basing trading decisions on a computerised statistical approach. As a result most of Trading Company's trading is based on analysis of price, volume and open interest as opposed to external factors of supply and demand. However, trading decisions will require the exercise of discretion by Trading Company. Discretion is required in the evaluation of trading methods used by Trading Company, and in their possible modification from time to time. The decision not to trade certain markets or not to make certain trades may materially affect performance.

Trading Company tracks and trades approximately 70 US and international futures contracts including foreign currencies, metals, interest rate futures, stock indexes, the energy complex and agricultural markets, although typically it will hold an average of 35 different positions.

Futures Ltd. engages in investment and trading in a wide range of futures markets. The objective of Futures Ltd. is to achieve the highest long-term return on capital consistent with principles designed to minimise the risk of permanent capital loss.

Futures Ltd. employs trading strategies developed by its principal who has been trading futures for his own account since 1977 and for customer accounts since 1981.

The trading strategy used by Futures Ltd. is based on two factors:

- a higher than average probability that a price move can be anticipated, measured and captured;
- the assignment of realistic definition and control upon initiating a market position.

Futures Ltd. utilises aspects of both technical and fundamental analysis in its approach to trading the markets.

Money Management Ltd. offers a discretionary trading service covering a number of commodity markets. Trading will be based on analysis of market trends and patterns combined with a knowledge of the underlying fundamentals of the commodity traded and will take into consideration any short-term influencing factors.

The two principal trading advisers have been employed in the futures industry for 12 years and 17 years respectively.

Money Management's trading approach is not limited to trend following or cyclical change analysis but allows for a mixed approach which creates the flexibility to respond quickly to changes in market conditions.

The Financial Fund

Investment Objectives

The objective of the Financial Fund is to achieve superior long-term capital appreciation through trading futures, options, spot and forward contract markets (futures) in any of the major international financial futures markets, including stock indexes, bonds and short-dated interest rates, currencies and precious metals.

The CTAS

Futures Managers Ltd. (profiled earlier)
Fund Co.
Trading Inc.
Trader

Fund Co. has been a US futures trading manager since 1972. Trading decisions are made by Fund Co. based upon two distinct proprietary trading systems. Both of these trading systems combine computerised, technical trend-following with quantitative portfolio management analysis. The principal objective of the trading systems is to profit from major and sustained futures price trends.

Fund Co. trades on all of the major US futures exchanges and has recently commenced trading in options on futures contracts and in forward contracts on the interbank market for foreign currencies.

Trading Inc. is a US corporation formed for the purpose of achieving capital appreciation through the speculative trading of futures.

The trading programme is systematic and technical in nature. However, Trading Inc. is not a chartist firm and will exercise its judgement and discretion in interpreting the signals generated by its trading programme. Trading Inc. will make decisions regarding the trading of futures, including selecting the markets which will be followed and those which will be actively traded, the contract months in which positions will be maintained and how they are to be traded.

Trading Inc.'s Arbitrage Programme is currently applied primarily to the financial markets. Trading Inc. generally seeks to determine whether a deviation in yield exists between different US treasury futures contracts. The arbitrage programme generally emphasises medium- to long-term position trading (from one week to three months).

Trading Inc. may trade Eurodollar futures contracts in conjunction with the Arbitrage Programme and may purchase and sell futures and options on futures of any commodity as part of the overall risk diversification programme. In addition, Trading Inc. applies similar strategies to futures contracts on the obligations of foreign governments which are traded on the international futures exchanges.

Trader became involved in the securities business shortly after he joined his bank in 1985. In 1986 he was responsible at the bank for the new stock options market and in 1988 he also assumed responsibility for the new stock index futures and options contracts.

He applies his trading system to the CAC 40 stock index and is developing other systems on different markets.

Trader uses a number of systematic trend following strategies which are technical in nature. These strategies are developed from an analysis of weekly, daily and hourly price charts. Trade initiations rely on the convergence of different technical indicators.

Initiations and liquidations of trades are always in the direction of the trend. The strategy is designed to let profits run and cut losses short. If a trend materialises, a stop will be placed to protect profits. In addition, predetermined stop/loss points are calculated for each trade.

The markets which may be traded by Trader include (but are not limited to): currencies, interest rates, stock indexes, precious metals and the oil complex. He reserves the right to trade in any futures contract, options on futures, stock options and stock index options. The first markets on which Trader intends to trade are the stock index and interest rate sectors, and particularly the CAC 40 stock index.

The Currency Fund

Investment Objectives

To achieve superior long term capital appreciation through trading in the international currency markets, using futures and options traded on the international monetary market (IMM) or other regulated currency exchange, and spot and forward contracts via the interbank market.

The CTAs

Subject to prevailing market conditions, the company has allocated The Currency trading assets to the following CTAs.

  Futures Managers Ltd. (profiled earlier)
  Cash Corporation
  Forex Fund Management Ltd.

Cash Corporation is a US corporation which was organised in 1982 to manage discretionary accounts in commodity and currency futures and forward markets. The business was originally established in 1971. Cash Corporation will trade a diversified portfolio of forward and futures contracts on currencies, including cross-rate positions. It may, in the future, trade currency options.

Trading decisions are made using a systematic trading method, which includes technical trend analysis (and certain non-trend-following technical systems), together with strict money management principles. The principal objective of the trading method is to participate in all major sustained price moves in the markets traded. The systems have been developed through actual trading experience and through computer testing against historical futures trading data.

Forex Fund Management Ltd. was incorporated in 1982 and is a wholly-owned subsidiary of a UK holding company. The Forex Currency System is a computerised, statistically based system which trades in the major international currency markets — primarily the currency futures and forward markets in the US, Europe and Japan. The objective of the system is to profit from exploiting exchange-rate fluctuations caused by a variety of market factors, including variations in interest rates, short-term technical adjustments and changes in the economic cycles of the world's principal economies.

The system is relatively long-term, the anticipated holding period for positions being between two and six months. However, in market conditions where interest-rate adjusted price trends do not occur, more frequent trading will take place.

CASE STUDY FOR FUND B

The Rationale Behind the Launch of a Managed Futures
Fund by a European Bank

To meet investor demands, fund sponsors, from pension funds to private banks, are increasingly buying in specialist expertise rather than attempting to develop their own managed futures investment strategies. Their aim, in an increasingly competitive environment, is to maintain client loyalty through the provision of innovative products and services designed to increase the assets under management and ensure consistency of performance.

International banks, are very well positioned to provide the specialist expertise demanded by fund sponsors. First, a large international bank is able to draw on the collective knowledge of many areas of financial activity from investment management through to transaction banking and futures clearing services. Second, and perhaps more importantly, a bank can provide principal protection or investor assurance in a variety of forms.

A guarantee of principal protection is an attractive solution for the cautious or cynical investor, since no matter what happens to the performance of a fund, the initial principal is protected. On the other hand, the life of a managed fund is traditionally five to seven years and some investors may not choose to invest a sum of money in a product which, over its life, may only return the initial investment.

The investor is thus able to lay off downside risk directly to a financial institution and at the same time benefit from a bank's established and well-developed risk management skills. Moreover, the bank's international knowledge and experience ensure that a particular fund's design can meet the needs of the investor, and trustee and regulatory requirements.

However, the provision of investor security in the form of a capital return guarantee is not, in itself, always sufficient to provide the level of investor 'comfort' or assurance which the fund sponsor requires. And it is important to understand that the guarantee element does not extend to any potential returns.

In administering managed futures products, major banks can also call upon their industry expertise to assess and select the most suitable trading manager and advisers on the basis of past performance, trading history and so on. This due diligence is a key factor to the ultimate success, or otherwise, of any fund.

Providing investor assurance, both in the form of, for example, a letter-of-credit-backed risk management model, and philosophically in terms of the portfolio design, implementation and administration of a futures product, is not cheap. Costs to a managed futures fund generally include an upfront placement fee, management and fund administration fees, broking commissions and incentive fees. However, the investor is able to balance these costs with the advantages of fully diversified futures and options trading with no risk to principal investment; industry expertise in professional trading and risk disciplines; and the benefits of an established global clearing, settlement and custodial (trustee) network.

For example, this particular bank's letter-of-credit-backed investor assurance programme was designed as a dynamic and flexible alternative to zero coupons. Since letter-of-credit(L/C)-backed risk management models enable the fund to be more highly leveraged it is potentially easier to maintain or restore the value of the portfolio. To date, the bank concerned has provided this type of assurance package to over US$ 1bn of managed futures products offered internationally by third party sponsors such as Dean Witter and Prudential Securities, trading managers including Commodities Corp. and trading advisers like John W. Henry.

More recently, the bank offered high net worth individuals the opportunity to invest in an offshore closed-end private placement—Fund B—through a limited company registered in the Cayman Islands. At its close in March 1992, Fund B had raised US$ 135m, attracting subscriptions from the Middle East, South America and Asia as well as Europe and the UK.

There were three key attractions for Fund B investors: a relatively small minimum investment of US$ 100 000, an unusually short tenure of three years and a letter-of-credit-backed investor assurance programme.

For more than 65 per cent of investors, Fund B was their first experience of a futures-based managed investment, and a survey of all investors listed these three features as key to their participation. In priority order these were the L/C-backed assurance programme (95 per cent); the low minimum investment (80 per cent); and the three year maturity (63 per cent).

The objectives of Fund B are straightforward: a strong investment performance giving capital appreciation through investment in commodity and financial futures trading on approved exchanges, including the CME, CBOT, Matif, Liffe, Comex, Nyfe, and others, coupled with investor security through downside risk protection and portfolio monitoring. Investor security has traditionally been achieved through the use of discounted zero coupon bonds which require some 60 to 70 per cent of the assets (for a five-year fund) to be set aside in these instruments to accrue to par at the maturity of the fund.

In a low dollar rate environment, however, an increasing percentage of total assets is required to meet capital assurance guarantees, reducing even further the trading assets of the fund—and this in turn reduces the profit potential.

Investor assurance in Fund B is provided through the bank's innovative L/C-backed Principal Protection Programme (PPP) for multi-adviser products, which enables a maximum of 70 per cent of assets including trading gains to be committed to futures trading. An irrevocable L/C issued on behalf of the trading manager provides capital protection to all units redeemed at maturity—subject to predetermined leverage policy and the bank's proprietary Collateral

Table 9.1 Benefit of Letter-of-credit-backed Programme

	Trading Assets ($)	10% Loss of Total Assets ($)	Fall in Trading Assets (%)	Return Required to Restore Initial Capital (%)
L/C	70m	10m	14	17
Zero	40m	10m	25	33

and Leverage Monitoring System (CLMS) which monitors the collateral and leverage of the fund on a daily basis.

The leveraging policy imposes limits on the amount of the trading portfolio which can be invested in a single margin, trading adviser, market segment or contract. On a daily basis, the CLMS monitors the collateral and leverage of Fund B, based on information received from both the investment manager and the futures clearer and relating to the value of trading and non-trading assets, the risk-free rate available in the market, the time to maturity and the value of the L/C.

CLMS ensures that the value of the assets, on a daily basis, is sufficient to repay the capital at maturity, assuming reinvestment at the prevailing risk-free rate, and determines the daily tradeable amount which can be invested in futures. If performance is satisfactory, up to 70 per cent of Fund B's assets will be available to trade by the CTAs. If not, dynamic deleveraging techniques will reduce the tradeable amount to avoid or reduce potential losses. The active risk management process incorporates the additional factor of a safety cushion calculated on the maximum historical daily loss. If, on any day, the value of the assets do not meet the L/C obligation including the daily loss cushion, the trading manager will be required to contribute a further margin (5 per cent of the initial subscription) for Fund B to continue to trade.

Table 9.1 illustrates the benefit of an L/C principal protection backed managed futures investment, assuming a fund with initial capital of US$ 100m.

With the exception of the actual trading of futures instruments, the bank is directly responsible for every other aspect of the placement. As the sponsor and placing agent the Private Banking Group was responsible for designing and marketing the Fund B offering around the world to potential investors. Following Fund B's launch, the bank acts as administrator, trustee and paying agent through its Bank (Cayman) Limited.

The London office created and manages the letter of credit assurance programme. The Bank Brokerage is the clearing broker for all futures transactions except spot and forward foreign exchange and the Bank in New York is the counterparty for interbank foreign exchange activities (although another bank could be appointed subject to pre-determined qualifying criteria).

The Selection of the Trading Manager

The Bank selected Trading Manager Inc., one of the leading US futures investment houses, as the trading manager for Fund B. Trading Manager Inc. was established specifically to design and manage futures investments by retaining experienced CTAs to trade in the futures markets and manages over US$ 190m through selected CTAs.

Recently, Trading Manager Inc. was selected as the largest of three trading managers to manage the US$ 100m of assets committed to the futures market by the US's Virginia Retirement System.

Trading Manager Inc. employs an extremely active fund management approach utilising qualitative and quantitative analysis of the performance and trading characteristics of individual instruments and the constant review of CTAs—the type of market environment in which each operates best, the way in which trades are carried out and so on. The success of a managed fund is determined by the ability to react quickly to shifts in market trends and requires an informed and aggressive management style.

The CTAs

For Fund B, Trading Manager Inc. selected a limited number of CTAs (initially six) with complementary strategies and specialisations to ensure a balanced trading approach. All and any of the CTAs can, however, be changed subject to individual performance and the prevailing market environment, and Trading Manager Inc. is responsible for their particular terms and conditions and importantly, for the payment of their fees and performance bonuses.

The advisers themselves utilise proprietary trading strategies combining systematic and discretionary approaches with fundamental or other forms of technical analysis. In terms of performance, Fund B is aiming to achieve returns, net of all fees and expenses, of around 18 per cent per annum. (Fund B's relative performance is measured against the Mar Index, the industry standard.)

While there is obviously no guarantee of future performance, the protections or safeguards put into place by the Bank and the Trading Manager Inc. still make the Fund B offering a very attractive proposition.

The Field of Investment

At present, around 52 per cent of the tradeable portfolio is invested in financial futures with the balance in commodities futures. Fund B invests in a broad range of futures markets including currencies, metals, financials, energy and agricultural products, and aims to capitalise on developments in all the world's economic sectors wherever and whenever they occur. Fund B's success depends upon the continual monitoring of the balance between trading capital and the high grade securities, and achieving more consistent returns from a balanced, lower volatility portfolio than might traditionally be expected from more aggressive non-guaranteed futures funds.

Fees

Fees for managed futures products vary widely. The fee structure for guaranteed multi-adviser funds is particularly complex since it involves a combination of fixed and transaction based costs: the management fee is an annual percentage of the tradeable amount excluding brokerage commissions. Brokerage commissions for large funds are generally lower than for individual managed accounts.

The trading manager also receives an incentive bonus as a percentage of any net new trading profits generated on a quarterly basis by each CTA. Additionally, there are trustee and administration costs calculated as a percentage of NAV, an annual letter of credit cost with additional service and monitoring fees, and transaction-based custody fees.

The Bank's fee structure for Fund B is an up-front placement fee; a fixed annual fee of 4 per cent; and a performance fee of 33 per cent of net new highs. As a percentage of equity the performance fee comes up at between 5 and 6 per cent, so the average annual cost on this fund is between 9 and 10 per cent.

10
The Outlook for Managed Futures Funds

The managed derivatives industry is, without doubt, still in its infancy. More developments and growth lie in its future than have happened in its past. Practitioners in the managed futures industry in Europe should not get depressed about how little headway they seem to have made, when they consider that unit trusts in the UK are 60 years old, and did not see huge growth in funds under management until the 1980s.

It must also be remembered that not only is the managed futures industry worldwide very young, it is also very small. This is a niche market with US$ 13–15bn, maybe US$ 21bn, under management. To put this into perspective, it may be helpful to remember that a single fund group such as Fidelity has US$ 153bn under management.

How to develop the managed futures industry to more substantial proportions is something that has occupied some of the best minds in this business for the past five years.

Until the recent development of a more formalised managed derivatives industry in Europe, much of the European lobbying came from the derivatives exchanges themselves, or, in the UK, the work of the Joint Exchanges Committee (now known as the Futures and Options Association and outlined in the Useful Addresses section at the end of this report). These institutions are working to achieve the regulatory or taxation changes essential to promote the direct use of their derivative products.

The result of all that good work was that the usefulness of futures and options for hedging purposes, at the very least, became accepted by even the most staid of institutional investors across Europe. According to *Global Investor*'s survey of European pension funds published in June 1991:

One in 10 pension funds cited the use of derivative instruments as their next innovation in investment strategy. In the UK, a recent change in regulations clarified the tax position on the use of futures by pension funds, allowing them to use futures and other derivatives in investment strategies for the first time. Where pension funds are externally managed, derivatives are likely to be used in tactical asset allocation (TAA) strategies. TAA involves using derivatives to make short-term value-adding moves in the markets without disturbing a fund's underlying asset allocation. Derivatives, however, may also be used to minimise risk as part of a hedging strategy[1].

The next stage of the campaign for supporters of managed futures is to get institutions to use managed futures programmes, rather than just direct investment in futures and options, for risk management in their portfolios. This will be a slow, uphill struggle during which the managed futures industry itself is going to have to face up to a few difficult changes.

The American market has barely started in that direction. In the 1980s companies such as Eastman Kodak, Alcoa and Amoco started to put some part of their pension funds into managed derivatives programmes and it is now estimated that around half of the 200 largest pension funds in the US invest in derivatives.

The most significant development for managed futures in the US in 1991 was the decision by the managers of the Commonwealth of Virginia's state retirement system to commit US$ 100m—of US$ 15.5 billion—to managed futures programmes. However, this 1991 initiative has not been followed by a stampede of other state pension managers, desperate to put their money into managed futures programmes.

The US's Mar has conducted a sample study of 30 of the United States and their involvement with managed futures.

It estimates that four US states are involved in or are close to making an allocation in managed futures—Virginia, Massachusetts, Illinois and Alaska. It considers that three have not considered managed futures: Alabama, Oregon, South Carolina. Nine states have 'looked into managed futures but have not acted to use it or have decided against it'—Connecticut, Indiana, Louisiana, Maine, Montana, New Mexico, Oklahoma and West Virginia. Two states are neutral, according to Mar, Florida and Pennsylvania. A further nine have sufficient futures exposure in their equity and fixed-income portfolios or overlay strategies (California, Colorado, Idaho, Kansas, Maryland, Nevada, Tennessee, Wisconsin and Texas). Finally, Mar has been told that three states—Georgia, Arkansas and Wyoming—are barred from considering a futures programme.

A recent survey showed that the California Public Employees Retirement System (Calpers) with assets of US$ 75 billion looked at futures for 'risk mitigation' rather than trying to make a higher return. Its goals were quite clear: hedging against currency risk and to invest the money earned from stock

---

[1]Reproduced by permission from *Global Investor* (a Euromoney publication).

dividends until that pool became big enough to manage in its own right. Calpers chose two managed futures/forex investment managers and is happy with the result.

The struggle for acceptance of managed futures has seen its first success in the UK primarily in the retail sector, with the arrival of legislation that permits the establishment of domestic managed futures funds. However, this success has been limited by what many see as restrictive regulations and the limitation of the authorised vehicle to the unit trust structure.

To date, only four firms have launched UK futures and options funds (Fofs): an insurance company, Legal & General, and two unit trust and fund management companies, John Govett & Co, Mercury and Fidelity. However, interestingly, one of the most successful retail products of all time in the UK is the higher income bond produced by Foreign & Colonial, which relies upon derivatives to achieve its income, but is not a futures and options fund per se.

In the institutional sector it is quite possible that there have been more significant investments in managed derivative programmes, but the inherently secret nature of institutional investors makes it difficult to quantify. We do know that most large firms use derivatives for hedging or for making asset allocation shifts—mirroring the desired position using derivatives, and then taking the actual position with the underlying portfolio over a more convenient time frame.

If managed futures are to achieve wider acceptance in Europe, their proponents will need not only to publicise and exploit the advantages of investment in these vehicles, but also to address and counter their perceived drawbacks.

MANAGED FUTURES—A MODERN BUSINESS

Managed futures investment is a modern investment business whose growth parallels the development of the investment industry generally. Modern futures exchanges are state-of-the-art electronic exchanges working on a truly global, 24-hour basis. The successful CTA employs sophisticated trading strategies, equally assisted by technology in carrying out his investment decisions. The mathematical brains behind many CTAs' trading strategies are working on theories that could eventually win Nobel prizes for economics.

In the US, the UK and Ireland, the concept of the prudent man is enshrined in law. This means that each investment decision taken by an institutional fund manager in the US, or overseen by a trustee in the UK or Ireland, has by law to be taken with reference to the question: 'Would a prudent man do this?' It cannot be long before a disgruntled investor in a pension fund which has not achieved the returns he would have expected over his working life (perhaps one retiring in late 1987 would have been a good example) starts a test case against his fund manager or trustee for not using managed futures to enhance— or, indeed, to protect—his portfolio. Once that happens, all fund managers will need to revise their opinion of managed derivatives.

PART TWO
REGULATION AND TAXATION

11
Regulation of Managed Futures Funds in Europe

Europe is taken here to mean those countries loosely bound together geographically as Europe, rather than necessarily members of the EC. The countries covered include Austria, Belgium, Denmark, Finland, France, Germany, Greece, Ireland (the Republic of), Italy, Luxembourg, Netherlands, Norway, Portugal, Spain, Sweden, Switzerland, United Kingdom.

The majority of the EC countries covered have no legislation for domestic managed futures funds and so where that is the case, the information given relates to the marketing of offshore managed futures funds within that jurisdiction.

The bulk of the information in this chapter comes from the work of two lawyers and two legal firms. First, the author has drawn on the work of Iain Cullen of Simmons & Simmons for the European Managed Futures Association. And secondly, Martin Cornish of M. W. Cornish, Batty & Co supplied additional information on offshore fund private placement and also provided the following information which examines the issues relating to the international marketing of futures, options and other derivatives funds (referred to collectively as 'derivatives funds') on a private placement basis. The author would like to thank both of these distinguished lawyers for their help in preparing Part Two.

The objective of Part Two is to assist a promoter of a derivatives fund in deciding where to concentrate market resources.

KEY ISSUES IN INTERNATIONAL PRIVATE PLACEMENTS

- understand local private placement rules;
- identify those countries with the fewest restrictions;

- market to 'professionals';
- use locally licensed agents or introducers.

Different Countries, Different Rules:
The International Marketing of Derivatives Funds

A major constraint on the ability of fund managers to market funds on an international basis is the lack of consistency between the laws and regulations of different jurisdictions. Despite a general reduction in barriers to international trade and investment over the last decade and steps towards establishing a common set of rules by the EC—the UCITS legislation outlined in Appendix II—regulation is largely determined independently by domestic authorities and there is no overall set of rules.

The result is a complexity of rules and regulations creating a regulatory environment which, despite some moves towards harmonisation in certain areas, is still far from the 'level playing field' accepted as the ideal for the efficient operation of these markets.

The Compliance Problem

Almost without exception, countries have rules which prohibit the marketing of derivatives funds to the public without some form of registration process (Germany is the most notable exception—see below). While it may be advantageous to seek authorisation and establish a domestic derivatives fund in compliance with local public offering and/or local listing rules (where possible), the complications of meeting detailed criteria in a large number of jurisdictions and the associated set-up and compliance costs are likely to preclude such an option. In most cases, the only viable route is to register the fund in a very limited number of jurisdictions and to take advantage of exemptions available for funds marketed selectively on a private placement basis in other jurisdictions. It is essential, therefore, to understand the issues relating to private placements.

Local Private Placement Rules

Notwithstanding the diverse treatment of the regulation of funds in different countries, it is possible to identify certain basic issues which need to be considered in respect of any particular country and which determine the level of regulatory compliance necessary in each case.

Public Offering/Private Placement

Most countries have either formal or informal rules distinguishing private from public offers of interests in funds. One exception is Germany, where the relevant legislation relates only to funds whose underlying investments are 'securities'. Many derivatives do not come within the definition of securities. If a derivatives fund is not classified as a securities fund, it can avoid all German registration and prospectus provisions. This does not mean that Germany has no marketing restrictions. The details of Germany's laws on unsolicited calls and gaming provisions are set out below in the section on Germany.

A Limited Group of Investors

Usually, an exemption is available from public offer registration and disclosure requirements if the fund targets only professional investors. However, the definition of 'professional investor' varies and is not always precisely defined. Some countries also permit marketing to 'sophisticated' investors or 'members of a restricted circle'. Sophisticated investors are not usually defined at all and the interpretation of what constitutes sophisticated is more a matter of convention, left to the discretion of the authorities concerned. A 'restricted circle' usually means a group of persons who have some connection, for example, as members of a club or possibly clients of a bank or broker. In addition, many countries impose an upper limit on the number of investors that may be approached without the offer being constituted 'public'. Some countries apply specific financial criteria which limit both the number of sophisticated investors that can be approached and those investors' ability to resell or distribute the shares or units. Other countries take other routes. Switzerland has no such rules and the Swiss regulator, the Federal Banking Commission, will not give any sort of formal ruling. At best these are 'guidelines' which can be deduced from experience and informal views.

In countries where private placement rules specify a maximum number of investors that can be approached, that number varies from between 10 and 20 (in the case of Switzerland) to about 300 (France). The most common figure is 50 (for example, Spain, Norway, Belgium, Denmark, Japan).

In some cases, existing clients can be approached without any restrictions and such approaches are not included in any maximum number otherwise specified. Other countries, including Luxembourg and Italy, do not specify a number but nevertheless indicate that the authorities will have regard to the number of investors (professional or otherwise) that are approached when assessing whether an offer is constituted 'public'. Countries which do not specify an upper limit, provided other restrictions are observed, include the UK, the Netherlands and the Republic of Ireland.

Local Licence Registration Requirements

In many countries, it is insufficient merely to observe the professional or sophisticated investor requirements outlined above. In addition to limiting the type or number of investors, it is often necessary to obtain some form of licence or approval from local authorities in respect of the fund and/or to market through a locally licensed broker. For instance, one example is the UK, which has extensive regulatory requirements relating to who can actually approach potential investors. Authorised people can approach a much wider range of investors in the UK.

Other examples of countries requiring locally licensed intermediaries include Spain, Belgium, Norway and Sweden. In Spain, the rules go further than requiring licensed intermediaries. Prior authorisation must also be obtained before commencing even a private placement. This includes disclosure of the proposed distribution and investor network.

Finally, it should be noted that in many cases, professional investors are required to be authorised themselves. In Italy, for example, investing institutions can only be approached directly if those institutions are licensed under the Italian SIM law (which came into force in January 1992).

Regulatory Prohibitions/Exchange Controls

It should not be forgotten that some countries continue to impose foreign exchange and other controls that effectively prevent residents from investing in any kind of offshore fund. In Western Europe, Greece is the only country to retain some form of exchange control. However, for comparison purposes only, in the Middle East, such restrictions apply in Israel and Saudi Arabia; South Africa has particularly strict controls; and certain Central and South American countries have similar restrictions. For instance, Mexican laws prohibit investment in any non-Mexican funds and provide that only Mexican institutions and brokers may deal in securities.

Nevertheless, in practice, investors resident in such countries may be permitted to invest in overseas funds—for example, if they have access to legitimate funds outside of the local jurisdiction and the transaction takes place offshore.

In summary, promoters of derivatives funds wishing to market internationally are faced with an array of rules and regulations. Fund promoters need to be aware of the regulatory environment in each target market. By identifying and targeting those countries imposing the least restrictions and marketing on a selective basis within local private placement rules, the fund's exposure to investors can be maximised. One way of achieving this objective and simultaneously increasing the fund's ability to access a wider range of potential investors is to build up a network of local agents or distributors. Not only are they likely to have the requisite licences to operate in the relevant jurisdiction but they may often be able to market to a wider client base than the offshore promoter could legitimately access itself.

Each country is now considered individually.

AUSTRIA

Economic data

Population (1991):	7.823 million
% of total population aged 15–64:	67.4
GDP (1992):	US$ 186.0 billion
GDP per head:	US$ 20 963
National saving as % of GDP:	13.2
GDP volume change 1992–91:	2.0 per cent
Turnover of Financial Market as % of GDP:	Statistics not available
Exchange rate per US$ in December 1992:	11.13 schillings
Long-term interest rate in December 1992:	7.56 per cent
Short-term interest rate in December 1992:	8.74 per cent
Historical information:	First fund in Austria was an international equity fund in 1956. Between then and 1969, all funds launched were domestic or international equity funds. 1969 saw the first bond fund. 1987 saw 'near money market funds' investing in short term bonds. 1980s saw the first funds aimed at the institutional investor.

Legislation

Austria has as yet no legislation for domestic managed futures funds. However, the regulations for the marketing of offshore funds within Austria are as follows.

Marketing Offshore Managed Futures Funds in Austria

Austria's financial services legislation was revamped on 1 January 1992 with the Capital Markets Act which requires that a prospectus be issued for any offer to the public in Austria of shares in an offshore futures fund. The public in this case is defined as any non-specified person.

An example of this definition is that if an Austrian bank were to offer shares in an offshore futures fund to the clients for which it acts as a fund manager, this would not constitute a public offer, whereas if such an offer were made to every person holding an account at the bank, this would be considered to be a public offer.

A copy of the prospectus must be filed with the Österreichische Kontrollbank at least one working day before the day on which an offer is first made in Austria, and the contents of that prospectus must comply with the requirements of the Capital Markets Act. The prospectus must also be in German.

These requirements are based on those outlined in the EC prospectus directive, because despite the fact that Austria is not yet a member of the EC, it is already taking the relevant EC directives into account when it draws up new legislation.

Intermediaries in Austria

The selling of shares in an offshore managed futures fund is classified as undertaking investment business and so the intermediary concerned has to be licensed under the Banking Act in Austria. Foreign intermediaries do not have to register as such, as long as they have no place of business in Austria, and as long as they do not actively solicit Austrian investors, only sending out prospectuses in response to enquiries received.

BELGIUM

Economic Data

Population (1991):	10.005 million
% of total population aged 15–64:	66.7
GDP (1992):	US$ 217.5 billion
GDP per head:	US$ 20 007
National saving as % of GDP:	11.5
GDP volume change 1992–91:	1.3 per cent
Turnover of Financial Market as % of GDP (1992):	81.3
Exchange rate per US$ in October 1993:	34.76 francs
Long-term interest rate in December 1992:	7.91 per cent
Short-term interest rate in December 1992:	8.71 per cent

Historical information: First fund in Belgium was in 1948.
                                           Fund legislation came in 1957.
                                           Money market funds came in 1988.

Legislation

In theory, Belgium is soon to have legislation allowing the marketing of domestic managed futures funds.

The laws governing the financial services industry in Belgium were modernised extensively with the enactment of the Law on Financial Transactions and Financial Markets on 4 December 1990. This law came into force on 1 January 1991.

The Structure of Belgian Funds

The law refers to both open-ended and closed-ended investment funds, whether 'fonds commun de placement' (FCPs) which have a contractual form, or the corporate 'société d'investissement'. (A more detailed definition of FCPs is provided in the section on France.)

When formed, these funds have to choose one of seven categories of allowed investments. As individual categories, these include investments in futures and options contracts on commodities, or on securities, stock exchange indexes and currencies. This means that as yet, there is no regulation for a fund investing in all types of futures and options.

A royal decree is required for the provisions of the law relating to domestic futures funds to be implemented and, at the time of writing, there seems to be no particular pressure to get this decree adopted. The decree would provide for the setting-up of managed futures funds, but probably only in the corporate structure in view of the equal protection afforded to creditors under the bankruptcy law, which would apply to companies, but not to other types of fund structure.

Funds which invest in either category of futures and options contract are allowed to hold cash for ancillary purposes and will be able to hold cash and securities as investments in their own right once the royal decree is in place.

Funds will need to have prior approval from the Banking and Financial Commission of the content of their prospectuses and all funds will need to be registered with the commission.

Shares in an open-ended fund may be and shares in a closed-ended fund will have to be listed on one of the four Belgian stock exchanges. The name of a fund will also have to show clearly the type of fund it is, whether open-ended or closed-ended, and which type of investments it can use.

Offshore Futures Funds

Offshore futures funds can apply to the Banking Commission for approval to market in Belgium, since the passing of the royal decree of 23 October 1991. To get the approval, the fund must be authorised in its home jurisdiction by a supervisory authority whose duty it is to ensure the protection of investors.

As with domestic funds, offshore futures funds registering in Belgium must invest either in futures and options contracts on commodities or futures and options contracts on securities—they cannot invest in both. Also, they may have to have a custodian—without one the Banking Commission can refuse approval.

There is limited scope for avoiding the approval procedure through marketing strictly on a private placement basis. The rules defining private as opposed to public offerings have recently been revised and impose very strict limitations on such marketing. Restrictions placed on private offerings of offshore funds extend to all telephone calls and correspondence relating to funds not established in Belgium. Previous client relationships are exempted, as is an operation directed only at banks, public credit institutions and certain other investing institutions approved by the Belgian authorities. In these cases, not only can the fund avoid registration, but the intermediary does not need to be a licensed Belgian intermediary.

DENMARK

Economic Data

Population (1991):	5.154 million
% of population aged 15–64:	67.5
GDP (1992):	US$ 142.7 billion
GDP per head:	US$ 25 271
National saving as % of GDP:	8.7
GDP volume change 1992–91:	1.2 per cent
Turnover of Financial Market as % of GDP:	Statistics not available
Exchange rate per US$ in December 1992:	6.116 krones
Long-term interest rate in December 1992:	10.20 per cent
Short-term interest rate in December 1992:	12.00 per cent
Historical information:	First fund in Denmark was in 1928. Funds became open-ended in 1962. Abolition of foreign currency regulations in 1984 saw some growth in foreign equity investments.

Act no. 85 on Mutual Funds of 12 February 1990 regulates open-ended investment funds in Denmark and it restricts such funds to investing in futures only for currency and other purposes associated with hedging against risk. However, closed-ended funds, established using the Danish investment company or limited partnership structures, are not regulated by the Mutual Funds Act. These funds are not subject to any specific investment restrictions or any authorisation or licensing requirement and as a result may be used as a vehicle for domestic futures funds.

Prospectus Requirements

If shares in a closed-ended fund are to be marketed to the public, a prospectus complying with detailed contents requirements must be filed with the Commercial and Companies Agency, a regulatory authority under the jurisdiction of the Ministry of Industry.

Marketing will be generally regarded as being to the public if addressed to more than 10 people who are not professional investors, unless the minimum investment is over DKr 300 000.

The prospectus will be published by the Commercial and Companies Agency in its electronic information system, usually within seven to 10 days. After this process, marketing of the fund can start.

Listings on the Copenhagen stock exchange can be arranged for shares in a closed-ended Danish investment company and also, in theory at least, for interests in a closed-ended Danish limited partnership.

Offshore Fund Requirements

Shares in an offshore closed-ended futures fund can be marketed to the public in Denmark as long as they comply with the same requirement to file a prospectus in the Danish language as apply to domestic closed-ended funds.

Registration with the Danish authorities can be avoided if a fund is marketed on a private placement basis. A private offer may take place if shares in a fund are offered only to:

1. 'legal entities whose business it is to trade securities' including brokers, banks and institutional investors who hold securities portfolios;
and/or
2. individual investors who purchase shares in an amount not less than DKr 300 000 (approximately US$ 50 000).

The Danish Act on Prospectuses does not specify a maximum number of professional investors to whom shares may be offered without constituting a public offer. As a rough guide, however, local authorities are not likely to view an offer as public if it is made to a maximum of 40–50 Danish investors, each with a pre-existing client relationship with the offerer, and most of whom are 'professional investors'.

The Rules for Intermediaries

There are no requirements for an intermediary selling an offshore futures fund in Denmark to have a licence or other approval.

FINLAND

Economic Data

Population (1992):	5.029 million
% of total population aged 15–64:	67.2
GDP (1992):	US$ 112.7 billion
GDP per head:	US$ 24 845
National saving as % of GDP:	– 0.1
GDP volume change 1992–91:	– 1.8 per cent
Turnover of Financial Market as % of GDP (1992):	46.0
Exchange rate per US$ in December 1992:	5.132 marks
Long-term interest rate in December 1992:	13.21 per cent
Short-term interest rate in December 1992:	10.68 per cent

Legislation

There are no regulations for domestic managed futures funds in Finland and under the Investment Funds Act of 1987, Finnish funds generally are not allowed to invest in futures or options contracts. A revision of the Investment Funds Act is being worked on at the moment which would allow investment funds to invest in futures and options for efficient portfolio management purposes.

Selling Offshore Managed Futures Funds

The Investment Funds Act does not apply to offshore funds and consequently not to offshore managed futures funds and so the sale of such funds is subject only to compliance with the provisions of the Securities Market Act of 1989.

This regulates the marketing of shares; it prohibits, in particular, the giving of false or misleading information and requires that investors be given enough information for them to be able to judge the merits of an investment in a fund.

An offer of shares in a foreign fund may be made in Finland on a private placement basis if fewer than 50 investors are approached in total. Such numbers must include no more than 20 professional investors. Professional investors are described in the Finnish Securities Market Act as 'companies or institutions having broad experience and background in the investment field'.

The Rules on Intermediaries

It is considered that if an intermediary sells an investment in Finland but has no office in the country and the actual transaction takes place outside Finland, he is not carrying on an activity that requires a licence.

FRANCE

Economic Data

Population (1991):	57.05 million
% of total population aged 15–64:	65.7
GDP (1992):	US$ 1335.6 billion
GDP per head:	US$ 21 022
National saving as % of GDP:	7.5
GDP volume change 1992–91:	1.8 per cent
Turnover of Financial Market as % of GDP (1992):	28.7
Exchange rate per US$ in October 1993:	5.605 francs
Long-term interest rate in December 1992:	8.14 per cent
Short-term interest rate in December 1992:	11.34 per cent
Historical information:	First fund in France was in 1945. Funds became open-ended in 1964.

Legislation

France is one of the few European countries that has legislation in place for domestic managed futures funds. It was first introduced in December 1988 (the 1988 Law), although not implemented until September 1989.

The original legislation has been amended and supplemented by a series of further laws, orders, decrees and regulations.

Fonds Commun de Placement

The legislation allows for managed futures funds to be set up only using the fonds commun de placement (FCP) structure. This is essentially a pool of assets which is jointly owned by the investors who have an undivided proportional interest in them.

An FCP is always an open-ended structure, managed by a manager with its assets held by a depository with a registered office in France. It is similar to the UK unit trust and the US mutual fund. A managed futures fund FCP is known as a fonds commun d'intervention sur les marchés à terme (FCIMT).

Portfolio Restrictions

A FCIMT must keep at least 50 per cent of its funds in liquid assets and certain short-term money market securities. These assets cannot be used to pay margin calls, but beyond that there is no restriction on the level of gearing within the fund.

A FCIMT may invest in futures and options contracts that are traded on any of the authorised markets. A list of these was published by the Ministry of Finance on 6 September 1989.

Investors in a FCIMT can be held liable for the debts of the FCIMT only to the extent of the assets held in the FCIMT (article 10 of the 1988 law). This means that the risk of margin calls made by a broker or fund manager of a FCIMT may fall on the broker himself.

Launching Requirements

Before launching a FCIMT to investors, the FCIMT must be approved by the Commission des Opérations de Bourse (COB). A FCIMT needs to have raised FFr 2.5m within 30 days of receiving the COB's approval before it can commence operations.

Listing a FCIMT's Shares

In theory a FCIMT's shares can be listed on the Paris stock exchange but so far the decree needed to set out the conditions with which an application must comply has not been issued.

Once listings are possible, a listed FCIMT will be required to intervene in the market to control the price of its shares to within 1.5 per cent of the price at which they could be redeemed by an investor.

Advertising and the FCIMT

The rules on advertising FCIMTs are particularly strict. Article 23 of the 1988 law specifically prohibits advertising of any kind designed to raise subscriptions for shares in a FCIMT which invests in futures and options.

Financial canvassing, as defined in Law 72-6 of 3 January 1972, is also forbidden. The term includes going to visit people at their homes, businesses or in a public place on a regular basis to recommend that they subscribe, purchase, exchange or sell shares or take part in share transactions. Writing or telephoning them or sending them circulars is also forbidden.

There is no distinction between institutional or private investors, nor between public or private offerings under these restrictions. However, one is allowed to advertise FCIMTs and their investment advantages in a general way. Guidelines for general advertising are provided in the COB's *Monthly Bulletin* 131 of November 1980.

The COB has also indicated that it is acceptable for a fund manager, banker or stockbroker to advise its clients on particular FCIMTs for whom it conducts discretionary investment management services.

Selling Offshore Managed Futures Funds

The consent of the French Ministry of Finance and of the COB is required in order to market an overseas fund to the public in France and this is rarely, if ever, granted. 'Private placements' of foreign funds incorporated in an EC Member State are permitted (that is without Ministry of Finance approval or registration with the COB) provided:

1. marketing is limited to institutional investors who purchase for their own account, as long as the total number of potential investors contacted is under 300 (this exception allows contact by telephone or circulars);
2. no form of advertising (as defined below) is used;
3. any intermediaries in France do not have the power to conclude contracts on behalf of the overseas fund.

If marketing is conducted (whether directly or through intermediaries) which results in more than 300 investors being contacted, this constitutes a public offering. Further, there should be no solicitation of other funds since any investment by another fund may result in the French authorities deeming that there had been a public offering (that is, indirectly to the investors in such a fund).

Solicitation (for example, the making of telephone calls or sending circulars) is generally prohibited. However, calls and mailings to a limited number of financial institutions and sophisticated non-financial institutions are permitted. Also, French banks and certain other financial institutions including stockbrokers and portfolio managers can recommend investments to existing clients without being considered in breach of the solicitation rules if they notify the authorities and make the relevant filings. Otherwise, their communication must be strictly limited to informing their clients of the existence of a new product.

Any specific form of advertising is likely to constitute a public offering. 'Advertising' includes advertising by any medium and includes the distribution of prospectuses or circulars. This means no public announcements or advertisements. Prospectuses, sales memoranda and other information should not be generally available. It is possible, however, to make a general announcement informing the public of the existence of a new product (without naming the specific fund), indicating the name of the person to contact for further information.

GERMANY

Economic Data

Population (1992):	79.82 million
% of total population aged 15–64:	69.5
GDP (1992):	US$ 1762.6 billion
GDP per head:	US$ 24 585
National saving as % of GDP:	9.9
GDP volume change 1992–91:	0.6 per cent
Turnover of Financial Market as % of GDP (1992):	33.4
Exchange rate per US$ in October 1993:	1.59 Deutschmarks
Long-term interest rate in December 1992:	7.40 per cent
Short-term interest rate in December 1992:	9.04 per cent
Historical information:	First fund in Germany was in 1950. Fund legislation came in 1957 and has remained in force ever since, with a number of amendments. German funds are dominated by bonds.

Legislation

The Capital Investment Companies Act of 1957 regulates domestic investment funds in Germany and this Act imposes a number of restrictions on the investment scope of such funds.

Investment in futures and options is limited very strictly to hedging purposes only. The only route to selling a managed futures fund in Germany is to use the offshore route.

Selling Offshore Funds in Germany

This is governed by the Foreign Investment Fund Act of 1969 (the Act) which applies to funds whose shares are distributed to the public, in its widest sense, in Germany and which invest in securities or real estate with the aim of spreading investment risk.

As a result an offshore fund which invests in futures and options and is specifically excluded from investing in securities or real estate falls outside the Act. This means that an offshore managed futures fund can be sold widely in Germany as long as it complies with the domestic marketing rules laid out in the Act against Unfair Competition.

'Securities' are not defined in the Foreign Investment Fund Act but are interpreted, under general principles, as meaning 'transferable certificates' of any sort. Thus, it is not the nature of the underlying instruments but the nature of the document representing the relevant instrument which needs to be considered. Since German futures contracts are not in fact transferable (because the contracts are traded on a back-to-back basis as in the US and the UK), they would not be considered to be securities.

It is therefore necessary to check the position with regard to the relevant instruments to be traded, once these have been identified. For example, although OTC stock index and other options on securities should not, as a matter of strict interpretation, be considered to be securities they are, in fact, treated as such by the German authorities.

It should also be noted in the case of foreign funds that the question of whether an instrument is a 'security' is determined according to the law of the country where the instrument is created rather than domestic German law. As a result, certain UK and US instruments may be deemed to be securities for these purposes. As above, it is necessary to consider the nature of the contracts to be traded if the fund is to avoid classification as a 'securities fund', thereby eliminating the need for registration (see below).

The Treatment of Guaranteed Funds

However, an offshore guaranteed futures fund, where the guarantee structure is provided through the acquisition of US treasury bonds or other high-grade securities, falls under the Foreign Investment Fund Act. The exception to this rule is where a fund buys just one treasury bond or several bonds with the same maturity date, interest rate and other characteristics because then the fund will not be considered to be investing in securities with the aim of spreading investment risk.

Funds Under the Foreign Investment Fund Act

Funds which fall within the provisions of the Foreign Investment Fund Act must first be registered with the Federal Banking Supervisory Authority and comply with the detailed provisions of the Act.

An offshore futures fund which incorporates a wholly-owned subsidiary company for the purpose of trading futures and options might be caught by the Foreign Investment Fund Act if it could possibly be deemed that the shares in that subsidiary are securities bought with the aim of spreading investment risk within the meaning of the Act.

Negative Clearance

It is not a statutory requirement but advisable for an offshore futures fund to obtain a negative clearance from the Federal Banking Supervisory Authority confirming that the fund falls outside the Foreign Investment Fund Act.

If such a clearance is not obtained, the Federal Banking Supervisory Authority could subsequently suspend the marketing activities of a fund while it checks that no breach of the Foreign Investment Fund Act has taken place.

Copies of a fund's prospectus and material contracts (in German) should be filed with the Federal Banking Supervisory Authority and negative clearance should be received within between six weeks and two months.

Further Clearance

Again, not a requirement but something that is usually done is to have a chartered accountant formally verify the prospectus or offering documents of the fund to ensure that they reach certain standards. Beyond that, the contents of a prospectus or offer document for closed-ended offshore futures funds may be required to comply with the Securities Prospectuses Act of 1990.

GREECE

Economic data

Population (1991):	10.269 million
% of total population aged 15–64:	66.8
GDP (1992):	US$ 79.1 billion
GDP per head:	US$ 6873
National saving as % of GDP:	6.2
GDP volume change 1992–91:	1.2 per cent
Turnover of Financial Market as % of GDP:	Statistics not available
Exchange rate per US$ in December 1992:	209 drachmas
Long-term interest rate in December 1992:	Statistics not available
Short-term interest rate in December 1992:	Statistics not available
Historical information:	First funds in Greece came in the 1970s. 1990s have seen a period of rapid growth for funds—12 launched in just over one year, 95 per cent investing in equities.

Legislation

There are strict exchange controls maintained by the Bank of Greece preventing the supply of foreign currency for the purpose of offshore investment. These controls have recently become more flexible in respect of securities listed on an EC stock exchange. However, in respect of shares in a company not listed on any stock exchange, the restrictions on foreign currency still apply. No doubt Greek exchange controls will be removed in due course when it becomes a full member of the EC but no specific timetable has been set for this.

Greek law provides that companies through which permitted transactions are made must be either Greek branches of overseas banks or financial institutions, or Greek registered offshore companies. In either case, some form of registration with the local authorities is required.

There does not appear to be a private placement alternative by which to circumvent either the exchange controls or the registration requirements.

IRELAND (THE REPUBLIC OF)

Economic Data

Population (1992):	3.6 million
% of total population aged 15–64:	61.8

GDP (1992):   US$ 48.8 billion
GDP per head: US$ 12 338
National saving as % of GDP: 13.8
GDP volume change 1992–91:   2.6 per cent
Turnover of Financial Market as % of
  GDP: Statistics not available
Exchange rate per US$ in December 1992:   0.599 punts
Long-term interest rate in December 1992:   Statistics not available
Short-term interest rate in December 1992:   Statistics not available
Historical information: Dublin's International Financial
                                                 Services Centre (IFSC) was
                                                 launched in 1987 to help create
                                                 jobs and redevelop a run down
                                                 part of Dublin's docks. It is a
                                                 special tax area and carries special
                                                 incentives for firms registered
                                                 there, and their products.

Legislation

The Unit Trusts Act 1990 and Part XIII of the Companies Act 1990, brought
in on 20 December 1990 and 1 February 1991 respectively, allow Irish unit trusts
and open-ended investment companies to invest in futures and options, not just
for hedging purposes but also as investments in their own right.

Authorisation of Managed Futures Funds

Managed futures funds must be authorised by the Central Bank of Ireland and
fulfil conditions including restrictions on investment, contents of their
prospectuses, supervisory requirements and reporting requirements.

Funds for Professional Investors

The Central Bank may lift its investment restrictions in the case of funds which
sell to professional investors only, and these are deemed to be funds which have
a minimum subscription of IR£ 200 000.

Listing Funds

A fund can list its shares on the Official List of the Irish unit of the International
Stock Exchange of the UK and the Republic of Ireland, as can an offshore fund.

Investment Restrictions

Managed futures funds are divided into 'capital protected' funds, also known as guaranteed funds, and 'leveraged funds'. Many of the conditions for authorisation of managed futures funds apply to both types. Funds can only invest in futures and options contracts which are traded on an organised exchange—although this is not defined—and off-exchange options are permitted if the counterparty has shareholders' funds in excess of IR£ 100m or equivalent.

A fund may neither hold an open position in any one futures or options contract for which the margin or premium represents 5 per cent or more of its net assets, nor may it hold an open position in contracts relating to a single commodity or financial instrument for which the margin requirement is ten per cent or more of net assets.

The Central Bank can also agree a derogation from these limits to allow a fund to achieve its investment objective of tracking the performance of a securities index.

Leveraged funds are subject to further conditions. The property of such funds must at all times include liquid assets which have a total minimum value equal to the amount of the sum of all margins deposited and all premiums paid in respect of transactions which have not been closed out.

These funds must also impose a minimum subscription of IR£ 10 000 or equivalent per investor, and their prospectus must contain a prominent risk warning about the risks involved in this type of fund plus a full description of those risks (this is also required for capital protected funds).

Capital protected funds must also be designed to provide protection of capital over no longer than seven years.

Offshore Futures Funds

An offshore futures fund cannot market its shares in Ireland without the prior approval of the Central Bank. If the fund is authorised in the jurisdiction in which it is established by a supervisory authority whose function it is to ensure the protection of investors and which provides a similar level of investor protection as that under Irish law, the fund can gain approval from the Central Bank.

Similarly, if the Central Bank is happy that the management and custodial arrangements, constitution and investment objectives of the fund are high enough to provide such a level of investor protection, it can grant approval.

ITALY

Economic Data

Population (1991):	57.114 million
% of total population aged 15–64:	69.0
GDP (1992):	US$ 1225.9 billion
GDP per head:	US$ 19 911
National saving as % of GDP:	6.7
GDP volume change 1992–91:	1.2 per cent
Turnover of Financial Market as % of GDP (1992):	16.0
Exchange rate per US$ in October 1993:	1574 lira
Long-term interest rate in December 1992:	12.31 per cent
Short-term interest rate in December 1992:	13.58 per cent
Historical information:	First funds were marketed in Italy in the 1960s but domiciled in Luxembourg. Legislation permitting domestic funds came in 1983. 1980s saw a period of rapid growth for funds which was overturned in 1987 and has not been seen again.

Legislation

Italy now has legislation which allows the marketing of offshore funds within the country. This is principally set out in the provisions of Law No. 86 of 27 January 1992.

Marketing Offshore Funds in Italy

To market offshore funds to the public, an application must be made to the Ministry of Treasury and the Ministry of Foreign Trade for authorisation. This will only be granted if these ministries are satisfied that the laws of the jurisdiction in which the offshore futures fund is incorporated are compatible with Italian law. The fund will have to open a representative office in Italy and will also have to either appoint an Italian bank or use a bank from another EC member state that has a branch in Italy that can act as custodian of its assets. Authorisation is deemed to have been granted if not refused within 60 days of the date on which the application was made to the Ministry of Foreign Trade.

Prior notice must also be given to the Commissione Nazionale per le Societa e la Borsa (Consob) that shares in an offshore fund are going to be offered, and a prospectus, prepared in compliance with the same rules that apply to Italian investment funds, must also be registered with Consob. Consob has 20 days after this event to require further information to be put into the prospectus, or to require that the offer be made in a different way.

The Bank of Italy must also be given advance notice. The Bank of Italy has 15 days in which to request more information and within 20 days it can limit the maximum amount of the offer or impose other conditions.

An offer to the public is defined in Law No. 216 of 7 June 1974 in extremely wide terms and so the structure of a private offer must be very carefully put together.

All securities and brokerage activity in Italy is now governed by the recently introduced 'SIM Law' (Societa di Intermediazione Mobiliare). A foreign firm marketing an overseas fund in Italy has to either deal through a SIM-licensed bank or broker to obtain a SIM licence itself. The licence requirements include Italian incorporation, and this can only be obtained by companies with majority Italian ownership.

The exact meaning of 'private' as opposed to 'public' solicitation is unclear. However, the status of investors (for example, whether they need protection) and the number of persons approached are relevant. In addition, there is a 'safe harbour rule' exempting certain transactions from the public offering rules if they are made to professional investors. For the purposes of this rule 'professional investors' means:

1. banks and credit institutions;
2. insurance companies;
3. companies managing mutual funds;
4. stock exchange brokerage companies;
5. financial companies.

Subsequent to any placement, Consob must be notified of the names of purchasing investors, the type of fund and the amounts involved.

The SIM law prohibits foreign firms from sending representatives to Italy in order to solicit new business directly or undertaking any form of advertising of its services. It does not prevent foreign firms dealing through SIM-licensed banks or brokers, who can then on-sell funds on a private placement basis (as outlined above).

It seems therefore that a foreign firm can make a private offering directly to the above professional investors provided those investors are SIM-licensed themselves. If the professional investors are not SIM-licensed (for example, insurance companies, mutual funds), the approach has to be made through a SIM-licensed broker. For the SIM-licensed institutions to on-sell the fund to the public, the standard approval process with Consob must be complied with.

Other exceptions to the licence requirements include unsolicited and independent approaches made by Italian residents and contact by a foreign firm which has an existing relationship with Italian clients.

LUXEMBOURG

Economic Data

Population (1992):	390 000
% of total population aged 15–64:	68.8
GDP (1992):	US$ 10.5 billion
GDP per head:	US$ 24 698
National saving as % of GDP:	48.7
GDP volume change 1992–91:	2.4 per cent
Turnover of Financial Market as % of GDP:	Statistics not available
Exchange rate per US$ in December 1992:	35.23 francs
Long-term interest rate in December 1992:	Statistics not available
Short-term interest rate in December 1992:	Statistics not available
Historical information:	First funds were registered in Luxembourg in 1959, under existing company law. In 1966 the current fund structures were introduced. 1983 saw the arrival of the FCP and the SICAF and SICAV. Luxembourg has seen exponential growth of its fund industry. Luxembourg dwarfs the other European offshore fund centres which have US$ 11 billion in assets under management.

Legislation

The law of 30 March 1988 allows investment funds to be established under Luxembourg law as either open-ended or closed-ended funds in both contractual and corporate form. The Luxembourg Monetary Institute (IML) is in charge of regulating such funds. In Circular 91/75, which was issued on 21 January 1991, the IML brought in new rules with which a managed futures fund must comply. Once approval has been achieved, the fund can obtain a listing on the Luxembourg Stock Exchange.

Investment Restrictions on Domestic Managed Futures Funds

The current rules on funds impose a minimum subscription requirement of LFr 500 000 per investor and impose various investment restrictions on managed futures funds. A Luxembourg managed futures fund may employ up to 70 per cent of its net assets for margin and option premiums, and so the fund can have quite a high level of gearing. However, this may not be increased further by borrowing and the balance of the funds must be held in cash and liquid assets. Furthermore, only futures and options contracts traded on an organised market may be used. To try to maintain diversification of risk, a fund cannot hold open positions in a single futures contract if the margin payable represents five per cent or more of the fund's net assets.

Also, no open position can be held in futures contracts relating to a single commodity or in a single category of financial futures contract if the margin payable represents 20 per cent or more of the fund's net assets.

The IML's prior consent is needed if a managed futures fund is to invest in a fund manager's or commodity trading adviser's own fund. This is because investment by one fund in another is normally limited to a maximum of ten per cent of the first fund's net assets. The IML can also give its approval to a managed futures fund of the guaranteed type which trades futures and options through a wholly-owned subsidiary company.

Since the Bank of Credit and Commerce International (BCCI) affair, the IML now also requires the promoter of a Luxembourg domestic futures fund to demonstrate that it has sufficient financial resources to make good any losses to investors.

Private Placement Funds

In July 1991, Luxembourg brought in legislation relating to private funds which are offered for sale to one or several institutional investors. Funds like this are now governed by the law of 30 March 1988, and so fall under the IML rules on futures and options funds. This means that institutional funds, such as pension or insurance funds, could invest in futures and options through a structured fund or even through an umbrella fund which could offer a range of asset classes.

Offshore Futures Funds

If the IML gives its approval, shares in offshore futures funds can be sold in Luxembourg, as long as they comply with domestic marketing rules on consumer protection and canvassing market practices. Approval will only be given if the offshore fund concerned is regulated, in the jurisdiction in which it is established, by a supervisory authority set up by law to ensure the protection of investors.

A private offering of an offshore fund can be made in Luxembourg without registering the fund or seeking a listing in Luxembourg. To qualify as a private placement, there must be no public solicitation or advertising in Luxembourg.

Offers may only be made to a limited number of institutional investors including banks, non-banking financial institutions, brokers, mutual fund agents and professionals engaged in the marketing of mutual funds and authorised as such in Luxembourg. There is no specific limit as to the number of investors to whom such a private placement can be made, although offers should not be made to other funds otherwise the offering will be deemed to be a public offering (that is, to all the investors of the fund). There are no unsolicited calls or similar rules.

THE NETHERLANDS

Economic Data

Population (1991):	15.07 million
% of total population aged 15–64:	68.8
GDP (1992):	US$ 323 billion
GDP per head:	US$ 19 298
National saving as % of GDP:	13.7
GDP volume change 1992–91:	1.4 per cent
Turnover of Financial Market as % of GDP (1992):	39.2
Exchange rate per US$ in December 1992:	1.778 guilders
Long-term interest rate in December 1992:	7.46 per cent
Short-term interest rate in December 1992:	8.66 per cent
Historical information:	First fund was established in 1774. It invested in foreign bonds and offered an alternative to the low interest rates available in the Netherlands at the time. 1920s saw more familiar structures.

Legislation

Investment funds are regulated under Dutch law by the Act on the Supervision of Investment Institutions (the ASII) which came into force on 15 October 1990. This law applies to both domestic and offshore futures funds. Both types of funds must obtain a licence from the Netherlands Bank before they can start marketing their shares in or from the Netherlands, unless the marketing is addressed solely to a restricted circle of prospective investors or to professional investors such as insurance companies, banks or pension funds.

Gaining a Licence

The requirements for a licence are quite wide, including giving information on the relevant expertise of the directors or managers of the fund, the share capital of the fund, its constitutional documents and a wide variety of other things. An application can take up to two to three months to be processed although it can be expedited if there is a valid reason.

Structures of Managed Futures Funds in the Netherlands

Such a fund can be an investment company or a mutual fund, either open- or closed-ended. These funds can, if formed as investment institutions, seek a listing for their shares on the Amsterdam stock exchange, although this could give rise to a separate tax problem.

Intermediary Legislation in the Netherlands

The Act on the Supervision of the Securities Trade of 1991 (the ASST) came into effect from 15 June 1992. Under the ASST, an intermediary who wishes to market shares in a licensed domestic or offshore futures fund in the Netherlands must obtain a full licence, unless the intermediary falls within certain exemptions.

These include an exemption for intermediaries who are members of one of the Netherlands securities exchanges and for promotion which is limited to a 'restricted circle of investors' including professionals, such as banks, pension funds, insurance companies, securities firms, investment institutions, central governments, large international and supranational organisations. Treasury and finance subsidiaries of large enterprises which are active on a regular and professional basis in the financial markets for their own account are also included.

In this context, a 'restricted circle of investors' means a group of individuals or legal entities which is precisely described or defined and which is limited in numbers. There must also be an existing relationship between the intermediary and the members of the group other than a financial relationship and the sales material must also make it clear that only the members of that particular group can apply for shares. The requirement for a relationship to be non-financial between the intermediary and group members prevents an unlicensed intermediary promoting a licensed futures fund to its existing customers since it is thought that the practical effect of this requirement is to limit the 'restricted circle' exemption to promotion among members of a club or society.

Beyond that, the exemption from the licence requirement for promotion to professionals is subject to the condition that any advertising or other promotional material, including the prospectus or other offering documents, must contain an appropriate selling restriction.

Also, a prospectus or other offering document which is to be distributed in the Netherlands under this exemption must be sent in advance to the Foundation for the Supervision of the Securities Trade to allow it to check that the selling restriction has been adhered to. However, the foundation does not have to approve the prospectus.

NORWAY

Economic Data

Population (1991):	4.61 million
% of total population aged 15–64:	64.7
GDP (1992):	US$ 112.6 billion
GDP per head:	US$ 24 854
National saving as % of GDP:	9.1
GDP volume change 1992–91:	2.9 per cent
Turnover of Financial Market as % of GDP (1992):	59.8
Exchange rate per US$ in December 1992:	6.674 krones
Long-term interest rate in December 1992:	9.18 per cent
Short-term interest rate in December 1992:	15.42 per cent
Historical information:	First fund was established in 1966, investing in equities. 1987 saw first money market and bond funds which are increasingly popular, over equities.

Legislation

Regulation for domestic unit trusts in Norway is set out in the Norwegian Unit Trust Act of 12 June 1981. Under this Act, unit trusts have to have an open-ended structure and a contractual form. They cannot be set up as an investment company.

Unit trusts in Norway cannot invest in futures. However, draft new provisions of the Act have been published which, if enacted, would allow Norwegian unit trusts to use exchange-traded futures for hedging purposes only.

Marketing of Offshore Futures Funds in Norway

The marketing of shares in an offshore futures fund in Norway is largely prohibited. If an investor approaches an intermediary and asks to invest in an offshore futures fund, the intermediary may help; but marketing using a prospectus, advertisement or other promotional material, including by way of a private placement, is prohibited.

PORTUGAL

Economic data

Population (1991):	9.814 million
% of total population aged 15–64:	67.0
GDP (1992):	US$ 83.4 billion
GDP per head:	US$ 6991
National saving as % of GDP:	21.1
GDP volume change 1992–91:	1.9 per cent
Turnover of Financial Market as % of GDP:	Statistics not available
Exchange rate per US$ in October 1993:	141.65 escudos
Long-term interest rate in December 1992:	Statistics not available
Short-term interest rate in December 1992:	Statistics not available
Historical information:	First fund was established in 1965. In 1976 all funds were nationalised and all participants were recompensed by the state. 1985 saw a new legal framework for funds. The market is dominated by money market and bond funds.

Legislation

Current legislation for funds in Portugal is based on the Decree-Law 229-C/88, and allows for the formation of both open-ended and closed-ended funds in contractual form.

Such funds cannot at present invest in futures, although a review of the legislation is under way to incorporate the UCITS directive, and this may allow the use of futures in domestic funds for hedging purposes only.

Marketing of Offshore Futures Funds in Portugal

There is no provision for the marketing of offshore funds in Portugal. It is thought that an intermediary wishing to market shares in an offshore futures fund in Portugal would require authorisation from the Bank of Portugal or from the Commissao do Mercado de Valores Mobiliarios and that such authorisation would only be granted to an authorised institution in Portugal.

SPAIN

Economic Data

Population (1991):	39.025 million
% of total population aged 15–64:	67.3
GDP (1992):	US$ 579.8 billion
GDP per head:	US$ 13 509
National saving as % of GDP:	10.7
GDP volume change 1992–91:	1.4 per cent
Turnover of Financial Market as % of GDP (1992):	53.3
Exchange rate per US$ in October 1993:	129.8 pesetas
Long-term interest rate in December 1992:	12.99 per cent
Short-term interest rate in December 1992:	15.16 per cent
Historical information:	First fund was established in 1958 but little growth in the industry until the 1990s when regulatory and tax changes made funds more appealing.

Marketing Offshore Funds in Spain

Spain's regulations for marketing offshore futures funds are set out in the

Securities Market Act of 28 July 1988 (the SMA) and its subsequent implementations by royal decrees.

The royal decree 1393 of 2 November 1990 provides that offshore funds may be marketed in Spain, whether through an offer to the public or a private placing, as long as evidence is provided to the Comision Nacional del Mercado de Valores (the CNMV) that the fund concerned is authorised in a country with equivalent investor protection.

In addition, the relevant regulatory authority in that country must provide a report on the fund to the CNMV which contains no adverse comments, while all applicable Spanish legislation must be complied with.

Prior authorisation must also be sought from the Ministry of Economy and Finance. Such an application may be rejected on the grounds that the marketing of the fund may have an adverse effect on the Spanish balance of payments, currency market or monetary policy.

There are additional detailed requirements for selling an offshore fund imposed under the SMA. These include notifying the CNMV of the proposed marketing and sending them copies of various documents.

It is thought that to date no foreign futures funds have been successful in obtaining CNMV authorisation to offer shares to the public.

A partial exemption from such requirements can be gained through taking the private placement route, defined as offers addressed exclusively to institutional investors who invest in securities on a professional basis and offers addressed to fewer than 50 investors, the total value of which is less than Pta 500m (approximately US$ 5m), provided that no specific advertising campaign is carried out.

Spanish residents wishing to make foreign investments have in the past been subject to certain exchange controls, including an authorisation procedure through the Foreign Transactions Office (FTO). These controls are currently being revised in order to allow a freer movement of funds internationally. Nevertheless, it is still necessary for the Spanish resident to make the investment through a Spanish bank. The bank (which is monitored by the FTO) holds certificates or other title documents representing the investment, and may levy withholding tax. Repayments or transfers are also liable to be taxed for capital gains.

SWEDEN

Economic Data

Population (1991):	8.617 million
% of total population aged 15–64:	64.1
GDP (1992):	US$ 245.9 billion

GDP per head:	US$ 27 498
National saving as % of GDP:	3.6
GDP volume change 1992–91:	– 1.2 per cent
Turnover of Financial Market as % of GDP (1992):	78.3
Exchange rate per US$ in December 1992:	6.886 kronas
Long-term interest rate in December 1992:	9.91 per cent
Short-term interest rate in December 1992:	10.58 per cent
Historical information:	First fund was established in the 1950s but the industry saw little growth until 1978 when a new type of fund with a built-in tax incentive was introduced in an effort to encourage the Swedes to save more. 1984 a further tax exempt scheme was introduced.

Legislation

Sweden's Mutual Funds Act of 1990 may be extended to include other types of funds in the future, but as yet there is no provision for domestic futures funds in Sweden.

Marketing of Offshore Futures Funds

Offshore futures funds can be marketed in Sweden without a licence but an intermediary needs authorisation from the Finance Inspection Board pursuant to the Act on Securities Trading. Provided the rules under the Marketing Practices Act of 1975 are complied with, there are no restrictions on the persons to whom offshore futures funds can be promoted.

A Swedish resident investor must, in accordance with Swedish exchange regulations, use a Swedish bank or broker for payment for the shares. The investor must also, if the investment is deemed to be a portfolio investment, place the share certificates on deposit with a Swedish bank or a broker either in Sweden or abroad. If no share certificates will be issued, the Swedish investor must ensure that the shares cannot be disposed of without such Swedish bank's or broker's participation.

SWITZERLAND

Economic Data

Population (1991):	6.792 million
% of total population aged 15–64:	68.3
GDP (1992):	US$ 242.2 billion
GDP per head:	US$ 33 819
National saving as % of GDP:	21.3
GDP volume change 1992–91:	0.2 per cent
Turnover of Financial Market as % of GDP (1992):	Statistics not available
Exchange rate per US$ in October 1993:	1.4 francs
Long-term interest rate in December 1992:	5.48 per cent
Short-term interest rate in December 1992:	6.19 per cent
Historical information:	First fund was established in 1930 and the industry saw something of a boom after the Second World War. Swiss appetite is for bond and money market funds.

Legislation

In December 1991, a first draft of a new Swiss law on mutual funds was presented to the Federal Finance Department which contains provisions which, if enacted, will substantially amend the current Swiss fund legislation and allow both domestic and offshore futures funds to be sold in Switzerland, to the general public.

The new law is expected to be in place by 1995. Its principal aim is to ensure investor protection, but not through a catalogue of restricted investments, more by setting personal and professional standards as high as possible. The disclosure documents for funds will need to provide more information than is currently required and custodian banks must be separate firms from the fund's managers. Fund managers will also have to redeem shares in an open-ended fund at any time unless it is a fund which has been established for no more than ten years, in which case the fund will not have to redeem its shares if they are traded on a stock exchange or if the fund manager or custodian bank acts as a market-maker. The draft new law also allows a wider investment field for domestic funds, including a new so-called risk fund which can invest in precious metals, commodities, warrants, options and futures.

Marketing Offshore Funds in Switzerland

Under the current law, a licence to market shares in an offshore fund to the public in Switzerland can only be granted to a Swiss bank or a Swiss branch of a foreign bank, although not in respect of an offshore futures fund. Under the new law a licence may be granted to any person, but only if an offshore futures fund is subject to home country control and its structure and investment policies are equivalent to those of Swiss funds.

Under the new law, offshore futures funds will be able to obtain a licence to promote themselves in Switzerland whether they are contractual or corporate. They will be exempt from the requirement to redeem shares at any time.

A fund may avoid these requirements by marketing strictly on a private placement basis. In this case, no licences are required by the fund itself or the broking intermediary. However, a fairly restrictive stance on the number and type of investors that can be approached must be employed. The following criteria are applied:

1. marketing should be restricted to a very limited number of investors in Switzerland (about 12), although the number may be expanded (to no more than 20) in the case of institutional investors having a pre-existing relationship with the seller—for example, a banking or other intermediary;
2. private investors must be sophisticated and meet defined financial criteria suitable to the investment in question;
3. investors should be fully informed of the nature and risks of the proposed investment;
4. the minimum investment should be substantial;
5. there should be no advertising, and prospectuses and other marketing material should not be available at public places.

UNITED KINGDOM

Economic Data

Population (1991):	57.649 million
% of total population aged 15–64:	65.1
GDP (1992):	US$ 1039.4 billion
GDP per head:	US$ 17 596
National saving as % of GDP:	2.7
GDP volume change 1992–91:	− 0.9 per cent
Turnover of Financial Market as % of GDP (1992):	29.2

Exchange rate per US$ in October 1993: 0.653 pounds
Long-term interest rate in December 1992: 8.84 per cent
Short-term interest rate in December 1992: 7.16 per cent
Historical information: First fund was established in 1931 and the industry saw swift growth. In 1935 the first flexible trust was introduced. The industry saw growth periods in the 1960s and the 1980s, with most trusts investing in equities.

Legislation

The limitations of UK law mean that the UK has no open-ended investment companies, and so the principal type of collective investment vehicle is the unit trust.

After a lengthy period of debate, the UK authorised unit trust has recently been allowed to invest in futures and options under the Securities and Investments Board (SIB) regulations issued on 15 July 1991.

The regulations allow two types of unit trust schemes investing in futures and options (including off-exchange options) leveraged and unleveraged, known as geared futures and options futures (Gfofs) and futures and options funds (Fofs).

Both types of funds may acquire transferable securities, hold gold — up to 10 per cent — and enter into forward contracts in gold and foreign currency. Both may purchase or write options and buy or sell futures on approved derivatives markets, and both can deal, in a limited way, in off-exchange options. Either type may invest up to 5 per cent of the value of the fund in certain other funds.

The Fof's exposure to futures and options is required to be 'covered' by the property or rights which it holds. Property for cover can include transferable securities, gold, certain matching derivatives, cash and near cash. The borrowing limit for Fofs is the same 10 per cent limit that applies to authorised securities funds but Fofs are allowed to be long-term borrowers.

Gfofs' investments in futures and options do not have to be covered at all, other than where acquired for efficient portfolio management purposes under the SIB regulations.

No more than 20 per cent of the value of the Gfof can be invested in 'initial outlay' on futures and options contracts. Initial outlay is defined by the SIB regulations to include all initial margin or premium payments for futures and options contracts, but excludes variation margin.

A further 10 per cent of the property of a Gfof may be used to purchase options in certain circumstances, while borrowing on either a short-term or a long-term basis is prohibited.

Marketing Rules for Fofs and Gfofs

The rules on marketing Gfofs are more stringent than those which apply to Fofs, because Gfofs are perceived to have a greater requirement for investor protection. The marketing rules apply to direct offer advertising, unsolicited calls, cooling-off periods, projections, past performance comparisons, risk warnings, valuation and pricing.

There is no legislation on guaranteed funds as yet, and Fofs and Gfofs are not allowed to pay performance fees. There is further debate in progress on the whole subject of authorised unit trusts investing in futures and options and the SIB is likely to make amendments to the original regulations by 1994.

Marketing of Offshore Futures Funds in the UK

The marketing of offshore funds in the UK is governed by the Financial Services Act 1986 (FSA) and the Financial Services (Promotion of Unregulated Schemes) Regulations 1991. The applicable rules are complex.

Offshore futures funds may not be promoted in the UK to the general public but may be promoted by authorised persons to, *inter alia*, the following categories of persons:

1. persons who are already participants in such a fund or who have participated in such a fund in the last 30 months;
2. persons in respect of whom the authorised person has taken reasonable steps to ensure that investment in the fund is suitable (after having sought information about their circumstances and investment objectives), and who are 'established customers' or 'newly accepted customers' of the authorised person or of a person in the same group;
3. permitted, authorised and exempted persons;
4. 'non-private customers' and persons who are treated as non-private customers.

12

Regulation of Managed Futures Funds in the Principal European Offshore Centres

This chapter covers the regulatory environment for managed futures funds in a selection of European offshore centres:

- Gibraltar;
- Isle of Man;
- Guernsey;
- Jersey.

GIBRALTAR

There are no specific regulations for futures funds in Gibraltar, but the Financial Services (Collective Investment Schemes) Regulations, 1991 apply to futures funds established in Gibraltar in addition to the Part III of the Financial Services Ordinance.

The regulator of the financial industry in Gibraltar is the Financial Services Commission (FSC) which may impose specific further requirements on particular funds under its discretionary powers.

Futures funds can be either open-ended or closed-ended, contractual or corporate. There are no specific investment restrictions, with the FSC deciding on each fund on a case by case basis. Depending on its decision, futures funds may invest in futures and options on or off exchange, and are not subject to any limit on the percentage of net assets which can be used for margin or option premiums and so on. General investment restrictions are set out in the regulations but the FSC prefers to take up a flexible approach with the emphasis on 'best practice'.

Approval from the FSC comes through a licence under regulations 4 and sections 6 and 8 of the ordinance. In order to obtain a licence, the marketing documentation must be submitted to the FSC, the manager of the fund must be a company incorporated and licensed in Gibraltar, and the applicant must complete a questionnaire and other documents.

It is likely that only persons or companies with a suitable track record in the futures fund business will be granted licences to operate from the Rock.

ISLE OF MAN

There is no specific legislation for futures funds in the Isle of Man. The Isle of Man Financial Supervision Act 1988 applies to collective investment schemes of all types. It allows for the formation of four classes of schemes: authorised, recognised, restricted and exempt restricted.

Futures funds are not allowed to be authorised schemes at the moment, and so domestic futures funds which are structured as collective investment schemes are either restricted or exempt restricted schemes. Restricted schemes are regulated under the Financial Supervision Act, while exempt restricted schemes are regarded as private arrangements and are not subject to regulation.

Closed-ended funds are not collective investment schemes as defined by the Financial Supervision Act and so are not subject to approval by the Isle of Man Financial Supervision Commission (FSC).

There are no particular investment restrictions for futures funds, but the FSC has stated that it prefers schemes whose primary investments are assets which can be easily liquidated and accurately valued through a recognised investment exchange or market.

Restricted schemes must have a manager in the Isle of Man who is authorised under the Investment Business Act 1991 and a trustee who is either an authorised person or who is authorised to act as a trustee under the law of one of the prescribed countries or territories, currently the UK, Jersey and Guernsey. The manager's licence must specifically apply to each restricted scheme it has to manage.

Exempt restricted schemes must have fewer than 50 investors and their constitutional documents must prohibit the making of an invitation in any part of the world to the public, or any section of it, to subscribe for or purchase shares in the scheme.

A closed-ended fund does not have to obtain any regulatory approval or licence from the FSC.

Any public offering by a futures fund in corporate form, including a closed-ended fund, must abide by the prospectus requirements of Isle of Man company law.

GUERNSEY (CHANNEL ISLANDS)

Futures funds can be set up in Guernsey as unit trusts or investment companies, either closed- or open-ended. Open-ended funds are regulated by the Guernsey Financial Services Commission (FSC) under the Protection of Investors (Bailiwick of Guernsey) Law 1987.

Closed-ended funds are regulated by the Advisory and Finance Committee under the Control of Borrowing (Bailiwick of Guernsey) Ordinances 1959 to 1989, although the FSC looks after all funds on a day-to-day basis.

Guernsey's FSC has a wide responsibility, including protecting and developing Guernsey's shares of the lucrative financial services industry. This means that only fund management businesses with pedigree and track record will be allowed to establish funds.

Open-ended futures funds are categorised in Guernsey as 'Class B' collective investment schemes and are governed by the Collective Investment Schemes (Class B) Rules 1990. These rules have a degree of flexibility which give the FSC discretion as to what conditions should be imposed on various schemes, taking into account particularly whether they are aimed at the retail, private client or institutional markets.

The Protection of Investors (POI) Law requires that every Class B fund has a designated manager and designated trustee or custodian and that these are different people and act independently of each other. They must also be incorporated, administered and have a place of business in Guernsey.

Closed-ended funds do not have these restrictions. They must instead obtain the consent of the Advisory and Finance Committee to raise money through the issue of shares.

JERSEY (CHANNEL ISLANDS)

Jersey funds are governed by the Collective Investment Funds (Jersey) Law 1988 and the Borrowing (Control) (Jersey) Law 1947 and the regulations and orders made under this legislation.

It is the Finance and Economics Committee in Jersey which has the power to control the establishment and regulation of Jersey funds and which exercises its power through the director of the financial services department (FSD).

Where a fund's offer of units or shares is to a restricted and identifiable group of not more than 50 persons who are in receipt of enough information to evaluate the offer reasonably, and where the units or shares will not be listed on a stock exchange within one year following the initial offer, these offers are regarded as private placements and will not be subject to regulation under the 1988 law.

The investment restriction rules on public futures funds in Jersey closely follow those relating to Fofs and Gfofs in the UK, but in Jersey they are more in the way of guidelines and there may be room for some degree of negotiation. Generally, the lower the minimum investment level in futures funds, the more severely the FSD's guidelines are applied.

Funds or their management will need track records in futures and each fund must have a management company and a trustee or custodian which are incorporated in Jersey and with an established place of business in Jersey.

Details on regulation for Dublin, Ireland and Luxembourg can be found under their country entries in Chapter 11.

13
Regulation of Managed Futures Funds in the US and Japan

In this chapter, brief details on the legislation for managed futures funds in the US and Japan are included, for comparison purposes only.

The US and Japanese information was supplied by Eric Bettelheim of Rogers & Wells; the author would like to thank him for his help.

THE UNITED STATES

The legislation for setting up and marketing managed futures funds in the US is incorporated in regulations from the Securities and Exchange Commission (the SEC), the Commodity Futures Trading Commission (the CFTC), and the securities (blue sky) laws of the 50 states.

Interests in funds are 'securities' under the Securities Act of 1933 and may only be offered or sold to the US general public in compliance with SEC rules. In addition, the organisers and advisers of derivative funds are generally required to register with the CFTC as commodity pool operators (CPOs) or commodity trading advisers (CTAs).

Funds whose principal activity is investing in equities and government securities must in most cases register with the SEC as investment companies (ICs) under the Investment Company Act of 1940 and their advisers are required to register with the SEC as investment advisers (IAs) under the Investment Advisers Act of 1940.

In order to avoid dual registration, US fund operators generally try to ensure that their investment policies do not bring individual funds within the regulatory scope of both the CFTC commodity pool and the SEC investment company regulation.

According to Eric Bettelheim of Rogers & Wells, the fact that there are a number of inconsistencies between the SEC and the CFTC regulatory systems, particularly with regard to the permissibility of performance-related fees, also militates against dual registration.

CFTC Regulation

The Commodity Exchange Act (CEA) gives the CFTC jurisdiction over transactions in futures, options on commodities and on futures, and options on futures on indexes of securities. This includes jurisdiction over those who organise, promote and trade for derivatives funds.

CPO Registration

Anyone who operates or solicits funds for a 'commodity pool', defined as funds trading in instruments which the CFTC regulates, is required to register with the CFTC. Any CPO operating on a commercial basis has to register unless the total within its funds is less than US$ 200 000 and no single fund has more than 15 participants. Certain entities such as insurance companies, banks and pension funds and ICs are exempt from the obligation to register.

A CPO has to become a member of the National Futures Association (NFA) and those of its staff who are involved in the futures and options business have to pass the National Commodity Futures Examination. Once registered, CPOs must comply with ongoing CFTC and NFA accounting, record-keeping and reporting requirements.

Unless it falls within the 'qualified eligible participants' exemption discussed below, every CPO has to file a disclosure document with the NFA and the CFTC. The purpose of this is to provide potential clients with the necessary information for them to make an informed decision as to whether or not to invest in the fund.

There are a large number of very detailed CFTC and NFA rules on the information about the fund and its principals which must be included in a disclosure document, particularly information on the trading policies and performance history. Trading performance must be disclosed in a specified format and CFTC-mandated risk disclosure statements must be clearly displayed. The disclosure document must also describe such matters as the way in which profits or losses will be allocated, restriction on transfer of interests, redemption procedures and frequency of account statements.

Each fund must have its own disclosure document and the CPO must send each participant in the fund a copy of the disclosure document before soliciting participation; it must also obtain a signed and dated acknowledgement of receipt of the disclosure document before accepting any money.

For CPOs based outside the US there are no special exemptions from CPO registration if they transact business directly with or for US customers in contracts traded on US exchanges. However, a non-US CPO operating a fund which trades solely in futures and options traded on non-US exchanges ('foreign futures and options') can avoid registration:

- if it does not have a US office, by appointing an authorised agent in the US for service of process;

or

- if it has a US office, if it is a member of one of the regulatory authorities in a number of countries, including France and the UK, which have reached exemption agreements with the CFTC, and by appointing a US agent for service of process.

A CPO located outside the US but trading US futures and options markets is exempt from CFTC registration as a CPO if it ensures that none of its funds' investors is a US resident or citizen and that no money is contributed from US sources.

CTA Regulation

Anyone whose business involves advising US citizens or residents on trading in CFTC-regulated contracts or who trades such contracts on a discretionary basis is required to register with the CFTC as a CTA and to become a member of the NFA. CTAs who have advised fewer than 15 people in the previous 12 months are exempt from registration if they do not publicly present themselves as CTAs.

The CFTC takes the view that if a CTA advises a fund, it advises each investor who participates in the fund and the CFTC counts each investor for purposes of its 15-person limit. If advice is only given in relation to pools for which a CPO is registered or exempt, the CFTC exempts it from the obligation to register as a CTA. CTAs must comply with CFTC and NFA membership application procedures and provide disclosure documents before soliciting clients.

The CFTC has recently adopted Rule 4.7, a 'qualified eligible participant' (QEP) exemption for CPOs and a 'qualified eligible client' QEC exemption for CTAs.

Rule 4.7 exempts registered CPOs from disclosure document filing and most reporting and record-keeping requirements in connection with fund interest sold solely to QEPs in private placements and other offerings (Exempt Pools) which are exempt from registration under the Securities Act of 1933. The Rule provides similar relief for registered CTAs trading for the account of certain QECs. There are four categories of QEPs, three classes of QEC and two categories which are both QEPs and QECs.

The following are for QEPs and QECs:

- Investment professionals, including registered futures commission merchants (FCMs) and broker-dealers, CPOs and CTAs with at least US$ 5m under management.
- Corporations, unincorporated entities and individuals owning or controlling a portfolio of at least US$ 2m in securities or which have deposited at least US$ 200 000 initial margin and option premiums for commodity interest trading (or a combination of the two). Beyond that, individuals must meet net worth criteria, while corporations and other entities must meet total asset size criteria.

The following are for QEPs only:

- Entities in which all of the equity owners are QEPs in either of the categories above.

The following are QECs only:

- Exempt pools.
- Entities whose sole owners are QECs.
- Insurance companies, banks, pension funds and ICs which are exempt from CPO registration whose sole owners are QEPs.

All promotional material which is sent to QEPs and QECs must contain a prominent statement pointing out that it is issued pursuant to the exemption. CPOs and CTAs, even if only dealing with QEPs, remain subject to the anti-fraud provisions of the CEA.

Securities Laws

Interests in derivatives funds 'securities' come under US federal and state securities laws, although the SEC does not have jurisdiction over trading in futures or in options on futures. Any sale of securities within, from or into the US is potentially regulated under these laws. Broadly, that means that for securities to be sold to the general public in the US by means of interstate commerce —

mailing, telephoning or travelling across state lines or into the US from abroad—a Securities Act registration statement, including a prospectus, must be filed with the SEC. The issuer of registered securities typically becomes subject to continuing reporting requirements under the Securities Exchange Act.

Beyond complying with the federal securities laws, the public offering of interests in derivatives funds requires separate registration or exemption under the blue sky laws for every state in which they are offered for sale. In many states the SEC filings may be used to achieve registration in routine fashion but in certain states regulators require additional information.

Offshore funds offered to the US public are usually subject to SEC regulation. SEC regulation S gives a limited exemption, allowing offshore funds to be sold to US citizens not resident in the US, and to be sold to US citizens provided that no 'directed selling efforts' occur in the US and that the offer and sale are made in an offshore transaction.

Offshore and other non-SEC registered funds can be sold through a private placement, (an offering of securities to a limited number of sophisticated investors) which is exempt from the Securities Act registration requirements. An offering made in accordance with the detailed rules in SEC regulation D is deemed to be private by the SEC.

Use of Derivatives by Investment Companies

As long as ICs comply with SEC regulations concerning asset coverage, there are no significant restrictions on their use of derivatives. However, an IC which uses derivatives more than just as a hedging strategy potentially faces the need to register with the CFTC as a CPO and may be required to comply with two different regulatory regimes.

Where an IC is registered with the SEC, its operator is not required to register with the CFTC as a CPO, if the IC enters into transactions in CFTC regulated derivatives for bona fide hedging purposes.

This exemption is dependent on the IC complying with the following conditions:

- it commits no more than 5 per cent of its total net assets to initial margin and option premiums;
- it is not marketed as a derivatives fund;
- prospective participants are informed of the purpose of and restrictions on the IC's use of derivatives.

JAPAN

For many years the regulatory environment for derivatives funds in Japan was unclear. This has now been largely resolved by the introduction of the Commodity Fund Law (CFL) in April 1991 and regulations under the CFL which have been in force since April 1992. Before the enactment of this law, conflicts developed between regulators with overlapping jurisdictions, largely the ministries of finance (MOF), international trade and industry (MITI) and agriculture, forestry and fisheries (MAFF).

- **MOF** is responsible for the regulation of financial companies, banks and securities dealers, and supervises the Japanese financial markets. In addition to CFL, MOF permits derivatives investment by securities funds, as long as at least 50 per cent of the fund's investments are in securities or securities derivatives.
- **MITI** regulates trading companies and the Japanese metals, energy and rubber markets.
- **MAFF** has been keen to encourage active domestic commodity futures markets for hedging purposes, and has sought ways to develop derivatives funds within its jurisdiction over the grain markets.

The Division of Supervision

Under the new CFL and its accompanying regulations, MOF will regulate funds which focus on securities and financial derivatives; MITI will cover those investing in primarily energy and base and precious metals while MAFF will look after those in agricultural commodities.

Investment Restrictions

The regulations from the three ministries follow broadly the same guidelines. Under them, 50 per cent of a derivative fund's assets must be invested in grains, energy or other commodity futures. A maximum of 30 per cent of the fund's value may be put up as margin or premium in overseas financial derivatives contracts, or other permitted financial derivatives. Funds are barred from using Japanese financial futures other than stock index futures and their investment in Nikkei-225 futures is restricted to one per cent of asset value. Beyond that, guidelines restrict investment in overseas stock index futures to 10 per cent of funds' assets.

Currently, the minimum investment in a derivatives fund in Japan is Y 100m. However, companies with a proven track record in the promotion of foreign derivatives funds may sell Y 50m investments. Although the fund promoter is permitted to repurchase shares in the fund, no secondary market is permitted at present.

There are regulations which require strict separation between brokers and advisers. Advisers which are 50 per cent or more owned by a futures broker cannot use that broker. The legislation and regulations also establish detailed ongoing capital, reporting and disclosure requirements for fund operators. Both Japanese companies and foreign companies with an office in Japan are eligible to register as fund operators.

14

Tax Implications for Managed Futures Funds in Europe

This chapter has been compiled with the help of Arthur Andersen, particularly Victor Levy of Arthur Andersen's Financial Services tax practice in London. It covers the taxation of futures funds and derivatives in a broader sense for the leading European markets. The author would like to thank him and the European offices of Arthur Andersen for their help.

BELGIUM

In Belgium, the law of December 1990 regulated in an extensive way the status of investment funds (initially covered by the law of 1957) and created two new types of investment companies: the SICAV and the SICAF. The SICAV is the société d'investissement à capital variable, while the SICAF is the société d'investissement à capital fixe.

The income that the investor receives from an investment fund is regarded as interest income but where the investment fund provides details of the underlying income distributed (for example, dividend and interest separately), each of these elements can be taxed according to its specific nature. On the contrary, the income distributed by an investment company will be qualified as dividend income and not as interest income.

The interest and dividends distributed to an investment fund are subject to withholding taxes which are not creditable nor refundable. Interest and dividends distributed by the fund are not subject to any withholding taxes.

This problem is now partially corrected by the royal decree of 18 January 1990, which states that Belgian collective investment funds are exempt from paying withholding taxes on their dividend income, provided they are recognised by the minister of finance, and also fulfil several conditions. Of particular importance is the requirement that the fund must invest at least 75 per cent of its assets in Belgian shares and that investors must subscribe to special certificates of the fund.

Taxation of Investment Companies

The Belgian SICAVs and SICAFs must be established in corporate form and as such they are subject to corporate income tax. However, special rules apply which mean that investment companies are taxed on the total amount of disallowed expenses and any specific advantages granted to investment companies.

Such income is taxed at normal rates (41 per cent for tax year 1991, 39 per cent for tax year 1992) and any reduced rates are not applicable.

Since investment companies are subject to corporate tax, they fall within the scope of the international double taxation treaties concluded by Belgium. Belgian investment companies are not subject to contribution tax on capital at their incorporation or in the case of capital increase.

Dividend Received Exemption

Investment companies are not entitled to the dividend received exemption since double taxation has already been excluded due to the special rules limiting the taxation of these companies in Belgium.

Further, commercial and industrial companies receiving dividends distributed by investment companies cannot claim the dividend received exemption unless the investment company proves that the dividends so distributed originated as 'qualifying income'.

Withholding Taxes

The income of the investment companies is subject to withholding taxes, which are creditable against the corporate tax of the investment company and refundable. However, foreign withholding taxes are not creditable against Belgian taxes.

Tax Credit and Foreign Tax Credit

Both regimes are not applicable to investment companies, so these credits are not included under the disallowed expenses.

Acquisition of Own Shares

Since the law of December 1989, the amount that exceeds the distribution value of the original holding is in principle considered as a dividend distribution. However, no taxes will be due, since these distributed profits are not within the scope of taxation.

Secret Commission

Investment companies are subject to a special tax regime on undisclosed commissions for unsupported payments (which are taxable at a rate of 200 per cent).

FRANCE

France benefits from favourable, although not perfect, legal and tax treatment for futures and options funds. Frederic Laureau, partner with Arthur Andersen's international tax practice in Paris, explains the current tax legislation.

The fonds communs d'intervention sur les marchés à terme (FCIMT) were brought into being by a 1987 law covering collective investment undertakings which operate on futures and options markets.

The FCIMT is an open-ended fund without legal personality and, although beyond the scope of the UCITS European directive, is subject to some of the rules which are applicable to French UCITS, as well as specific legislation.

FCIMTs have no explicit rules governing non-taxability. Nevertheless it is generally considered that as FCPs, FCIMTs are beyond the scope of French income tax. As far as private investors are concerned, recent legislation has clarified and softened the relevant tax rules. FCIMTs are deemed completely transparent, as if the investor in the fund were carrying out transactions directly on the futures markets. This means that the profits arising from the fund's transactions are taxed to the investor, as far as he participates in the fund, in the year they are realised. As a consequence of the 'transparency rule', it makes no difference whether or not the profits are effectively distributed by the fund.

Provided that the investor does not, apart from his participation in the fund, intervene on futures markets on a regular basis, he will be regarded as an 'occasional operator' for French tax purposes. As such, the income he receives from the FCIMT will be taxed at 16 per cent (in practice, actually 18.1 per cent because of additional taxes) if it derives from transactions on French futures markets.

If the profits have been realised on foreign futures markets the low taxation scheme should not be applied. Where this is not applicable, the corresponding income would be taxable at progressive rates (up to 56.8 per cent). Losses incurred by the fund can be offset against other profits of the same kind and carried over for a period of five years.

Should the investor be regarded as a 'usual operator' on the futures markets, the income received from the FCIMT will be taxed as non-commercial profits at progressive rates (up to 56.8 per cent). Losses incurred can be offset against profits of the same kind and carried over for a period of five years.

No specific rules have been issued so far on how corporate investors are taxed. Nevertheless, administrative comments on the taxation of profits realised on futures markets by ordinary FCPs are generally considered to be transposable to FCIMTs.

As for individual investors, these rules provide for the 'pass through' principle. Consequently, corporate investors, members of a FCIMT, could be treated as if they had directly operated on the futures markets. Thus, the gains realised by the FCIMT, whether reinvested in the fund or distributed, could be taxable in the hands of the investor, up to the level of his participation in the fund, under the same rules as those applicable to direct transactions on futures markets.

In conclusion, the main rule governing the taxation of FCIMTs is transparency. As some consider that this pass-through principle is likely to hamper further development of FCIMTs, the adoption of a capitalisation fund regime for French futures and options funds might be commendable in order to complete the range of France's investment opportunities.

GERMANY

At the time of writing there are no futures funds in existence in Germany. The German national law does not provide for the establishment of futures funds. With the implementation of the EC directives as national law, effective as of 1 March 1990, the legal framework for UCITS in Germany has been altered. Ordinary mutual funds may invest in futures within certain limitations. However, the establishment of a fund investing 100 per cent in futures is not possible even under the provisions of the new laws.

IRELAND (THE REPUBLIC OF)

Futures funds in Ireland can be set up as unit trusts, variable capital companies or trading companies. Unit trusts and variable capital companies are transparent for tax purposes, generally speaking, while trading companies are subject to a ten per cent rate of tax where they engage in particular certified activities.

Unit trusts and variable capital companies that make payments to Irish resident unit-holders are obliged to deduct tax at the standard rate, currently 27 per cent, on those payments.

LUXEMBOURG

There are no special rules for managed futures funds other than those prevailing for other investment funds. Investment funds located in Luxembourg are exempt from all taxes except a flat capital contribution tax on incorporation of LFr 50 000 and an annual subscription tax of 0.06 per cent on the fund's aggregate net assets.

No withholding tax is applied on the distributions from a fund.

Due to this liberal tax status, the application of double tax treaties to Luxembourg investment funds has generally been denied by various other European tax authorities.

In 1992, the director of the Luxembourg tax administration confirmed that the revenue is prepared to issue the certificate of residence which may be required for the application of various treaties to Luxembourg SICAVs or SICAFs, that is, investment funds organised as Luxembourg limited companies. Indeed, at that time, the revenue authorities of Austria, Finland, Germany and the UK indicated that they would apply the treaty to Luxembourg investment companies.

However, it seems that at least two of the above-mentioned countries, namely Germany and the UK, have revised their initial position and continue to deny the application of the relevant treaty provision to income derived by Luxembourg investment companies.

THE NETHERLANDS

The legal entity in the form of a NV, BV or joint investment fund may under a number of conditions qualify for a special tax status.

Generally, the character of a joint fund may be either open or closed. The character of the fund can, for Dutch purposes, substantially influence the tax treatment of such a fund.

A closed fund is transparent for Dutch tax purposes, so all benefits accruing to the fund are directly taxed at the level of the participants. Closed investment funds as such are therefore not individually subject to taxation in the Netherlands. An open fund, on the other hand, is a corporate entity which in principle is subject to corporate income tax at rates of 40 per cent and 35 per cent, unless the fund qualifies as an investment fund.

Based on the special tax incentive for qualifying investment funds, an investment fund is not a tax-exempt vehicle but is subject to corporate income tax at a rate of zero per cent, provided a number of conditions are met. The philosophy behind this exemption is that, under certain circumstances, an investment entity has no purpose in itself, but is only a flow-through vehicle for the shareholders which should not generate an extra tax burden.

Conditions for Application of the Special Status

A company qualifies as an investment entity if the following conditions are met:

1. The company (a NV or BV or fonds voor gemene rekening) is resident in the Netherlands.
2. The statutory as well as the actual object of the company must be the investment of equity.
3. The loans obtained, if any, may consist only of:

    • mortgage loans on real estate, not exceeding 60 per cent of the book value of the immovable property;
    • any other loans not exceeding 20 per cent of the book value of the other investments.

4. Within eight months of the end of the book year, the fiscal profit must be distributed to the shareholders (or in the case of a joint investment fund to its participants).
5. The profit of the investment entity must be distributed equally on all shares. An investment entity needs the approval of the ministry of finance for the issuance of preferential shares.

Quoted Investment Entities

Special conditions apply to investment entities quoted on the Amsterdam stock exchange. In this respect an investment fund will be considered to be 'quoted' where the company is officially listed on the Amsterdam stock exchange.

In order for such a fund to qualify, 45 per cent or more of its stock may not be held by one company, or companies associated therewith, which are subject to corporate income tax.

Furthermore, additional conditions have to be met for directors and commissioners of a quoted investment fund. This test is introduced to avoid the situation where a fund meets the 45 per cent shareholders test, but through statutory directors/commissioners the actual vote of the company is transferred to a non-qualifying entity.

In the event that the fund is owned 25 per cent or more by a company or a group of related companies, then a director of such a fund is not allowed to hold concurrently the function of statutory director and be employed by such a company.

Also, the board of commissioners is not allowed to consist to the extent of over 50 per cent of persons who are at the same time directors or commissioners of a company holding an interest of 25 per cent or more in the fund.

Non-quoted Investment Institutions

If the company is not officially listed on the Amsterdam stock exchange, it is required (besides the general conditions as mentioned above) that at least 75 per cent of its shares be held by individuals and/or companies not subject to or exempt from corporate income tax and/or investment institutions officially listed on the Amsterdam stock exchange.

Non-resident Shareholders

In addition to the above-mentioned conditions for both quoted and non-quoted investment funds, a further provision applies to non-resident participants of such funds. In the event that the shares of an investment institution are held by non-resident shareholders, it should be noted that no non-resident shareholder (or participant), either individual or corporate, is allowed to own 25 per cent or more of the shares (participants).

On the other hand, residents of the Netherlands, whether corporate or individual, are not allowed to own 25 per cent or more of the shares in the company through non-resident companies or non-resident investment funds.

Taxation of an Investment Fund

If the above conditions are met, the company is subject to Dutch corporate income tax at a zero per cent tax rate. One of the major requirements to obtain this special tax status is that the profits of the company should be distributed within eight months of the taxable year. As a result the company will still have to compute a distributable income.

Capital gains made by a Dutch investment fund can be credited to a reinvestment reserve, from which certain releases should be made each year:

1. A reasonable remuneration should be made for the management of the investment fund.

2. Given the applicable limitations to the reserve, a possible available excess should be distributed.
3. A possible capital loss should also be released from the reserve.

Income derived from securities (dividends, premiums, interest), either national or foreign, is effectively not reported. Income from securities, as opposed to capital gains, should be included in the distributable profit of the investment company and therefore should be distributed within the eight-month period.

Although the investment company does not pay any tax, due to the zero per cent rate, it may be entitled to 'tax credits' for foreign withholding taxes where the shareholders/participants are Dutch residents. The credit is granted as a direct payment to the investment company.

Upon the distribution of both a qualifying investment company and an open fund dividend, withholding tax at the statutory rate of 25 per cent should be withheld, unless a treaty provides otherwise.

The investment company is not entitled to the Dutch participation exemption; nor does the investment company itself qualify as a participation.

Taxation on Individuals

Capital gains made by resident individuals are in general not included in the taxable income. Distributions of profit, on the other hand, will constitute taxable dividend income. The dividend withholding tax of 25 per cent is creditable against the income tax liability.

It should be noted that resident individual taxpayers are eligible for a DFL 1000 exemption of dividend income. This exemption is doubled for married couples.

Individual shareholders are not taxable on undistributed income accruing to the investment company. Where profits are not distributed within eight months, they are taxed at the level of the investment fund at the statutory rate of 40 per cent/35 per cent. Moreover, the fund will lose its privileged tax status as of the taxable year in which the fund fails to meet the conditions.

Profits which are credited to a generally accepted fiscal reserve will not have to be included in the taxable income of the year in which the fund loses its special status.

The amendment of the Investment Institutions Decree in 1990 means that the special status can apply to more qualifying investment entities, although subject to a large number of conditions. Even in the event that an investment entity invests in options and/or futures, the investment entity will be subject to corporate income tax at a zero per cent rate, provided that it fulfils all the conditions.

PORTUGAL

There are currently no funds in Portugal which invest in futures and options. As such there is no specific tax legislation in Portugal dealing with managed futures funds. It is, however, conceivable that when such funds become a reality, they will operate within the existing tax and regulatory framework established for portfolio investment funds. These enjoy tax exemption in respect of income or gains that have not been subjected to Portuguese withholding tax. Their distributions of income and gains to participants/unit-holders in the fund carry a tax credit for the withholding suffered by the fund on the underlying income.

To date, however, these funds have concentrated exclusively on shares and bonds and there is, as yet, no developed derivatives market in Portugal.

SPAIN

A specific tax regime for financial futures and options has not yet been developed in Spain, nor is one expected in the short term. Considering the general principles of the Spanish direct taxation system, we suggest the following highlights regarding their tax treatment:

- Income or loss from trading in financial futures and options may be considered a capital gain/loss for tax purposes and consequently would not be subject to withholding tax at source. Apart from the withholding issue, under Spanish tax rules a distinction between capital gain/loss and current income/loss is relevant only for individual taxpayers (gains could be partially exempt depending on the generation period and losses may be deductible directly only against capital gains).
- As a general rule, the tax effects of trading in these instruments do not appear until such time as the contract is settled. However, provisions for unrealised losses may be tax deductible under some circumstances. Furthermore, if profit and loss from hedging transactions are deferred in the accounts, they may both be deferred for tax purposes.
- Non-residents, whether individuals or corporations, trading on Spanish options and futures markets would not be taxed in Spain unless they were residents in a non-EC country with which Spain has no fiscal convention. Otherwise, tax at the rate of 35 per cent applies.

SWITZERLAND

Currently, Swiss funds can use futures and options only for hedging purposes, although the law is under revision, with the new version expected by 1993–94.

Swiss funds are regarded as transparent for tax purposes and as such are not subject to any Swiss income tax, but Swiss withholding tax of 35 per cent is imposed on distributions. In an effort to clamp down on roll-up funds, investors are also deemed to have received profits accumulated in growth funds in the year those profits are realised by the fund and thus credited to their accounts.

Swiss individuals pay no capital gains tax on items included in their private wealth, except for residents of the Canton of Grisons. This means that the use of futures and options in funds is particularly attractive because the gains realised on these transactions distributed to or accumulated in a fund escape Swiss taxation.

The lack of flexibility in Swiss funds, and the adverse tax consequences which these funds present to foreign investors, mean that foreign investment funds are more popular with the Swiss financial institutions. However, even with foreign funds, Swiss financial institutions have to face added Swiss tax costs which force them to seek much higher profitability in their investment transactions in order to compete in the international markets.

The extra costs come from the levying of a Swiss securities tax. Swiss financial institutions are deemed to be securities dealers for the purposes of the securities transfer tax. If the financial institution acts as an intermediary on the purchase and sale of units in foreign funds, the likelihood is that a securities transfer tax of 0.3 per cent will usually be due and payable as follows:

- half of the tax due (0.15 per cent) by the investor;
- the other half (0.15 per cent) by the foreign fund.

Under certain circumstances, part of the tax due may be avoided. An intermediary on a securities transaction is broadly defined as including any institution which indicates an opportunity to the parties to conclude the transaction. It is difficult for Swiss financial institutions to avoid falling within the terms of that definition.

The Swiss tax authorities also have taken the position that switching between funds in an umbrella fund is a taxable event for purposes of the securities transfer tax.

UNITED KINGDOM

The principal collective investment vehicle in the UK is a unit trust scheme and the taxation treatment will depend on whether it is an authorised or unauthorised vehicle. Until 1991, it was not possible to have an authorised vehicle investing in futures and options. However, since then Fofs and Gfofs have been accepted by the Securities Investment Board.

An authorised fund is subject to tax at 25 per cent on its general income which must be distributable to unit-holders. Capital sums may not be distributed but contribute to the growth of the fund and may be subject to capital gains tax on the disposal of the investment units by the investor. Credit is usually available for the 25 per cent tax suffered in the fund.

Income derived from transactions in futures and options contracts by an authorised unit trust is exempt from taxation. In addition there is an accounting complication, in that, for accounts purposes recommended practice suggests that futures and options 'income' should be treated as capital. The consequence of this is that where futures and options transactions operations are profitable, the 'correct' tax treatment is achieved as the receipts are excluded from taxable and distributable income. However, where the futures and options contracts give rise to losses, a mismatch occurs. In this case, there is no relief for the futures and options losses which are in the balance sheet and therefore not available to reduce the taxable and distributable income. For the investor, the income subjected to tax may be greater than the fund's net return. Given the potential volatility of futures and options funds year on year, this can be a considerable disadvantage.

UK Tax Implications for Managed Futures Funds Offshore

As one of the biggest centres for managed futures funds in Europe, the UK's treatment of such funds for tax purposes has caused particular concern.

The UK tax rules for fund managers running managed futures funds have been unclear for some time. The Statement of Practice issued on 29 November 1991 in the UK, entitled *The Treatment of Investment Managers and Their Overseas Clients*, came as a result of extensive lobbying from accountants working in the futures industry. The effect of the statement was to clarify the views of the Inland Revenue (IR) on a number of issues affecting investment management.

The principal one was whether a UK futures broker undertaking discretionary fund management could be regarded as an agent for a non-resident client and so liable for the UK tax on profits of a non-UK resident investor. So potentially serious was this problem that at least one UK fund management firm is believed to have moved its entire futures management operation to Switzerland.

The statement explains how and when a broker performing investment management services is protected from 'the agency risk' and so is exempt from assessment on the profits realised by the non-resident client.

The conditions that need to be observed to obtain this protection are as follows:

- the agent concerned should be carrying on a business providing investment management services to several clients including the non-resident in question;

- the investment transactions need to be carried out in the ordinary course of business;
- the remuneration received by the agent from the client is not less than the normal rate;
- if such profits or gains are taxable in the UK, the agent carrying out the investment transaction is also the agent through which the trade is carried on.

Victor Levy of Arthur Andersen provides the following example, which first appeared in the *Futures and Options World Directory & Review 1992*.

Example

Assume that a futures fund is set up in a tax haven, such as the Cayman Islands, where investors place sums of money to be handled by a manager resident there. In turn the manager appoints a related UK commodity trading adviser (CTA). The question to consider is whether the UK CTA can be safe from any threat of taxation under the agency rules.

Typically, the offshore management company manages the futures fund and the investors agree to pay an annual management fee of, perhaps, 3 per cent and an incentive fee of 20 per cent. The offshore management company appoints a number of CTAs who compete based on levels of fees and past performance. This would be the normal commercial practice since the offshore fund manager has to manage a number of individual accounts and there is additional administrative work. He can then pass a block of funds to the CTA to manage.

On the assumption that the UK CTA is a related party of the Cayman Islands fund manager, and that their level of charges are lower than those being charged to the investor, there is a potential tax problem. Although there is nothing untoward in this scenario, from a tax viewpoint the statement of practice states that to receive 'agency protection', the UK manager must effectively act in its affiliate's shoes and *for the same reward.*

In the situation outlined above, the UK CTA is not receiving the same reward as the offshore fund manager. There is no commercial reason why the domestic CTA should be entitled to receive the same reward as the overseas related manager, but there may well be an exposure to tax under the 'agency' provisions because the reward condition is not met. An unrelated CTA would probably not be affected by this rule.

The way in which arrangements are structured could be crucial. Documentation is also critical. For instance, the removal of the brokerage element from the discretionary fund management charge is a useful planning point.

For example, the non-resident fund manager could agree with the investors a commission rate of US$ 60 to US$ 80 per futures contract. The manager then negotiates with a broker a lower charge, of say US$ 15 to US$ 25 per contract. It will readily be appreciated that the fund manager could make a significant profit from this.

If the offshore fund manager decides to appoint a broker in the UK who is a related party, the brokerage activity, from a tax viewpoint, is dealt with totally separately from the discretionary fund management activity.

There is then no question of the IR attempting to link these two activities and the 'same reward' conditions do not apply. In other words, the tax risk on this part of the activity can be removed.

APPENDIX A
Rules for Trustees of Managed Futures Unit Trusts in the UK

As the UK has one of the most developed markets for domestic managed futures funds in Europe, the UK's rules for trustees are given here in the belief that they may indicate how other countries will treat domestic managed futures funds, once the regulatory problems have been solved.

Under the Financial Services (Regulated Schemes) Regulations 1991 made by the Securities and Investments Board, it is the duty of the trustee to retain control of all the property of the scheme while it is the manager's right and duty to make decisions as to the constituents of the property of the scheme. This includes making decisions in relation to derivatives transactions.

In this respect derivative transactions, excluding off-exchange derivatives, are no different to transactions in stocks and shares. The fund manager makes his decision and undertakes the transaction, the trustee reviews the transaction and if it is inappropriate will request the fund manager to unscramble it.

As with transactions in stocks and shares, there is no requirement for the fund manager to pre-advise derivative transactions, except off-exchange derivatives, but it is his duty to undertake all transactions within the regulations.

Where derivatives transactions will differ from transactions in stocks and shares is that there will be an ongoing requirement to ensure that all transactions remain fully covered at all times. In addition, some derivatives transactions will involve the pay or receipt of margin. An exception to the cover requirement is Gfofs.

APPENDIX B
Managed Futures and the UCITS Directive

UCITS stands for the undertakings for collective investment in transferable securities. It is the Council Directive of 20 December 1985 (85/611/EEC) and it provides for the establishment of collective investment schemes — funds — which can be marketed across the Community.

The original UCITS products are quite restricted as to which investment fields they can use, and the use of derivatives specifically was quite limited indeed. Article 21 of the UCITS Directive states:

1. The Member States may authorise UCITS to employ techniques and instruments relating to transferable securities under the conditions and within the limits which they lay down provided that such techniques and instruments are used for the purpose of efficient portfolio management.
2. The Member States may also authorise UCITS to employ techniques and instruments intended to provide protection against exchange risks in the context of the management of their assets and liabilities.

In 1990 there was clear confirmation from the EC that it meant to extend the UCITS directive, and as a result in July 1991 the Joint Exchanges Committee (the JEC) and the European Managed Futures Association (EMFA) presented a proposal to amend UCITS to allow the inclusion of futures and options funds.

At the same time, the European Federation of Investment Funds and Companies, of which the UK's Unit Trust Association (the UTA) is a member, also put in a proposal which included a recommendation for a limited type of futures and options fund.

The arguments for the inclusion of futures and options from the JEC and EMFA's point of view was that:

- The Investment Services Directive provides an EC 'passport' to investment firms in relation to direct trading by retail customers in futures markets. It must follow therefore that, in view of the well-documented fact that collective investment schemes are safer for the retail sector than direct position trading, such a 'passport' should be made available in relation to futures and options funds.
- The principal competitor jurisdictions to the EC, namely Japan and the US, both have liberalised the trading of futures and options funds for the retail sector.
- One of the objectives of establishing a Single European Market is to remove the things that increase the cost of doing business and impede innovation and growth; and that managed futures funds should be included in the amended UCITS now, because of their growth and popularity, rather than causing a later further revision.

The Commission called two meetings of the member states in February and May 1992 to consider the proposed amendments to UCITS, and found that there was a pronounced aversion to the inclusion of futures and options funds in UCITS by the majority of the member states.

As a result, it is unlikely that UCITS 2—which is expected but nobody quite knows when it will be published—will contain regulations allowing the establishment of pan-European managed futures funds. It may, however, allow the use of futures for tactical asset allocation, which may offer some comfort to the supporters of the managed futures industry in Europe.

Observers of the Commission feel that while the Commission itself was quite aware of the commercial potential of futures and options funds, it preferred not to get into a protracted argument with the member states on the subject.

Bibliography

Allen, G. C. *Managed Futures: An Institutional Investor's Primer*.

Baratz, M. S. *The Investor's Guide to Futures Money Management*. LJR Communications Inc., 1989.

Brorsen, B. Wade and Irwin, Scott H. Futures Funds and Price Volatility. *Review of Futures Markets*, 6(1987): 119–135.

Chamberlain, G. *Trading in Options*. Woodhead-Faulkner, 1990.

Commission des Opérations de Bourse, *Monthly Bulletin* 131, November 1980.

Courtney, D., and Bettelheim, E. C. *An Investor's Guide to the Commodity Futures Markets*. Butterworths, 1986.

Epstein, Charles. *Managed Futures in the Institutional Portfolio*. John Wiley & Sons, New York, 1992.

Euromoney *Dictionary of Derivatives*, 1992.

Gastineau, G. L. *Dictionary of Financial Risk Management*. Probus Publishing, 1992.

Group of Thirty *Derivatives: Practice and Principles*, 1993.

Lintner, John. The potential role of managed commodity-financial futures accounts (and/or funds) in portfolios of stocks and bonds. Paper presented at the annual conference of the Financial Analysts Federation, Toronto, Canada, May, 1983.

London International Financial Futures Exchange *Futures & Options Funds: New Opportunities*, 1991.

Managed Futures Association "Performance Measurement: Views on Evaluating the Returns of Managed Futures Investments," *The MFA Journal*, 1993.

McMillan, L. G. *Options as a Strategic Investment*. The New York Institute of Finance Corp, 1986.

Meaden, N., and Fox-Andrews, M. *Futures Fund Management*. Woodhead Faulkner (Publishers) Ltd., 1991.

Northcote, T. *Major Events in the History of the Managed Futures Industry*. The Managed Futures Association, 1993.

OECD *Organisation for Economic Co-operation and Development in Figures*, 1993.

Peters, C. C. *Managed Futures: Performance, Evaluation and Analysis of Commodity Funds, Pools and Accounts*. Probus Publishing Company, Chicago, 1992.

Sarnoff, P. *Trading in Financial Futures*. Woodhead-Faulkner, 1985.

Schwager, J. D. *Market Wizards: Interviews with Top Traders*. New York Institute of Finance Corp, 1989.

Useful Contacts

Callan Investments Institute 71, Stevenson Suite, Suite 1300, San Francisco, CA 94105, USA
Tel: 415 974 5060
Fax: 415 512 0524
Contact: Gregory C. Allen for copy of *An Institutional Investor's Primer*

The Commodity Futures Trading Commission 2033, K Street NW, Washington, DC 20581, USA
Tel: 202 254 6387
Fax: 202 254 3061
Acting director: R. David Gary

M. W. Cornish, Batty & Co. 11, Old Jewry, London EC2R 8DU, UK
Tel: 071 600 0910
Fax: 071 600 0837
Contact: Martin Cornish

The European Managed Futures Association International House, 1, St Katherine's Way, London E1 9UN, UK
Tel: 071 265 3688
Fax: 071 481 8485
Contact: Florence Lombard

The European Managed Futures Association was launched in September 1990 in Montreux, Switzerland. Its remit was to pursue the following objectives:

- To promote managed futures, options, forwards and other derivatives as an asset class and to provide advice and support services to its members.

- To offer its special expertise in the process of formulating regulations which will affect managed futures and options funds in Europe.
- To promote and protect members' interests.

Recently, EMFA has been involved in specific lobbying activities: lobbying national delegations to include managed futures in an expanded version of UCITS; working on the development of a directory of managed futures in Europe; the establishment of an official training course on managed futures and, finally, developing with its sister organisations The Japanese Commodity Fund Association and the Managed Futures Association, a committee to investigate and create a benchmark of performance for managed futures funds. The EMFA founding members list contains some of the leading individuals in the European managed futures industry:

David Anderson, Managed Futures Association
Anthony Belchambers, Futures and Options Association
Iain Craigie, Fund Management Financial Services Ltd. (Dublin)
Iain Cullen, Simmons & Simmons
Bill Dykes, RM Ravarumaklarna AB (Stockholm)
David Elkin, Credit Lyonnais Rouse
Martin Emery, Sweden (UK) Ltd.
David Hirshfield, Daiwa Europe Ltd.
Gerard Jwema, Shearson Lehman Hutton (Monte Carlo)
Victor Levy, Arthur Andersen
London Commodity Exchange
Prism Asset Management Ltd.
Shearson Lehman Brothers Inc. (London)
Adam Parkin, John Govett & Co. Ltd.
John Parry, Rostron Parry (London)
Henry Pollard, LPS Marketing Ltd. (Gibraltar)
Micky St Aldwyn, E D & F Man International Ltd.
Anthony Rucker, Federation of Commodity Associations
Bob Siebenmann, Balfour Maclaine International (UK) Ltd.
G. Stanley, Paine Webber International Futures
Jonathan Steiner, Steiner & Cie (Switzerland)
Ronald Thompson, Rosenthal Collins Group
Christopher Tilley, Bank in Liechtenstein (Geneva)
Volker Triebel, Droste Killius Triebel (Dusseldorf)
H. J. Th van Stokkom, Limako Brokerage NV (Breda NL)
Peter Wildblood, The International Petroleum Exchange of London Ltd.
Alain Zaquin, Shearson Lehman Hutton Inc. (Paris)

Current EMFA members

A & L Goodbody	Michael Greene
ADL Matif	Arend-Jan Huurneman
Adler Jansen Braun AG	Roland Jansen
Allingham Anderson Roll Ross	David Anderson
AMT Futures Ltd.	Derek Adler
Anglo Dutch Investments	David Oxley
Arendt & Medernach	Claude Kremer
Arthur Andersen	Victor Levy
Banque Internationale a Luxembourg	Pierre Jond
Bearbull Asset Mgmt	Francois Gillieron
Buchanan Capital Mgmt	Kevin Rowe
BVT Beratungs	Harald von Scharfenberg
BZW Futures	Graham Newall
C Wave Capital Mgmt Corp.	Marc Cohen
Campbell & Co. Mgmt Ltd.	James Little
Cargill Investor Services	James Davison
Chang Crowell Mgmt	Bruce Nelson Terry
Chicago Board of Trade	Peter Donnelly
Chicago Mercantile Exchange	Julie Murray
Citco (Suisse) SA	Luc Vuurmans
Citibank NA	Sohail Jaffer
Clifford Chance	Timothy Herrington
Colorado Commodities Mgmt Corp.	Tom Kellerhals
Comfitrade SA	Samir Jallaledine
Commodities Corporation (USA)	Robert Easton
Court Master & Co.	Carl Fink
Credit Lyonnais Rouse	David Elkin
Daiwa Europe Ltd.	David Hirshfield
Denton Hall Burgin & Warrens	Robert Finney
Droste Killius Triebel	Michael Leistikow
Dubin Swieca & Loze	Bernard Loze
E D & F Man International Ltd.	John Kelly
Eclipse Capital Mgmt Inc.	Thomas Moller
ECU Futures PLC	John Royden
ECU Terinvest	John Royden
Elton Int NV	Teunis Zuurmond
EQT-Cantatore SA	Jean Pierre Cantatore
Estlander & Ronnlund	Martin Estlander
European Investment Managers	Jonathan Steiner
European Investment Managers	Erika Bocherau
Ferri SA	J-F Conil-Lacoste
FFM Finanz AG	Helmut Beyer

Fintech Asset Mgmt	Donald Lewis
Foreign & Colonial Mgmt Ltd.	John Monkton
Fund Mgmt Financial Services	Ian Craigie
Fundservices International	Barry Herman
Futures & Options World	David Setters
Futures and Options Assoc.	Anthony Belchambers
Gandon Fund Mgmt Ltd.	Michael Cullen
Geldermann Inc.	Dirk DeBoer
GEMS	Gershon Shtekel
Gerald House	David Hands
GNI Ltd.	John Burridge
Goldschmidt Conseil & Associes	J Bernard Doliner
Hurlimann Urech & Uhlmann	Daniel Urech
Hassenbichler Trading Services	Gerrit Rath
Hunter & Co.	J. Laurie Hunter
ICCON GmbH	Thomas Cornelius
Indosuez Carr Futures Inc.	Didier Varlet
Intereffekt Futures BV	Mr Van Breeden
International Petroleum Exchange	Peter Wildblood
IQ Portfolio & Risk Mgmt AG	Ricardo Cordero
John Govett & Co. Ltd.	Adam Parkin
Joint Exchanges Committee	Anthony Belchambers
Kenmar International	Peter Huri
Kiefer & Partner	Rene Kiefer
Lehman Brothers	Alan Brody
Lehman Brothers	Alain Zaquin
Limako Futures Fund Mgmt BV	Henk van Stokkom
London Commodity Exchange	Robin Woodhead
London Securities Exchange	Lynton Jones
LPS Futures Managers	Tim Ireton
Lyon Ellis & Davis Ltd.	Tod Davis
Managed Derivatives	Beverly Chandler
Matif SA	Patrick Simonnet
Mees Pierson	Brian Wilkinson
MEFF Renta Fija	Juan Antonio Ketterer
Merrill Lynch	Hans Christian Koltze
Metallgesellschaft Corp.	Sabine Stechl
MI Capital Mgmt SA	Gerard Iwema
Midland Global Markets	Robert Coughlin
MKS Capital Mgmt	Jean Francois Liess
Mocatta Commercial Ltd.	Seamus O'Connell
Moore Capital Mgmt	James Kelly
Nat West Bank PLC	Victoria Ward

Paine Webber Gestion SA	Laurent Bensimon
Panholzer Advisory Corp.	Peter Panholzer
Pragma	John Alban
Providence Capitol	Kevin Carter
Prudential-Bache Futures Ltd.	Susan Casey
Rand Financial Services Inc.	John Wynn
Refco Inc.	Amy Coty
Rostron Parry	John Parry
RPM Risk & Portfolio Mgmt AB	Bill Dykes
Rudolf Wolff & Co. Ltd.	Ian Morley
Sabre Fund Mgmt Ltd.	Peter Swete
Schnelle & Partner	Ingo Schnelle
Schwarzkopf & Assoc.	Henning Schwarzkopf
Sentinel Mgmt Group Inc.	Eric Bloom
Servisen Financial Services	Dan Stridsberg
Silver Knight Investment Mgmt	Mark Shipman
Simmons & Simmons	Iain Cullen
Swiss Commodities Futures	Paul-André Jacot
Steiner & Co.	Jonathan Steiner
Sucden (UK) Ltd.	Martin Emery
Sydney Futures Exchange	David Chin
Tass Mgmt Ltd.	Nicola Meaden
Townley & Updike	Michael Griffin
Transtrend BV	G. Van Vliet
Trebor Financial Inc.	Robert Stein
Trendlogic Associates Inc.	Charles Dolan
Tricon USA Inc.	James Gaffney
Ulster Investment Bank	David Conway
Wagru Handels	Gero Biesel
Yield Enhancement Strategists	Shira B. Pickholz

The Futures Industry Association 2001, Pennsylvania Avenue NW, Suite 600, Washington DC 20006, USA
Tel: 202 466 5460
Fax: 202 296 3184
President: John M. Damgar

Futures and Options Association Roman Wall House, 1–2 Crutched Friars, London EC3N 2AN, UK
Tel: 071 488 4610
Fax: 071 696 9562
Executive Director: Anthony Belchambers

The Futures and Options Association, (FOA) was formed on 29th June 1993 and has taken over and expanded from much of the work done by the Joint Exchanges Committee. The JEC now serves as a forum for the exchanges to discuss and progress matters of common concern or of concern to their members or to the industry generally. Exchanges represented on the JEC comprise Liffe, the LME and the International Petroleum Exchange (IPE).

It has also been agreed that the FOA will provide the UK representative for EMFA.

Managed Account Reports Inc. 220, Fifth Avenue, 19th Floor, New York, NY 10001, USA
Tel: 212 213 6202
Fax: 212 213 1870
President: Greg Newton

Managed Account Reports Inc. Park House, Park Terrace, Worcester Park, Surrey, KT4 7HY, UK
Tel: 071 827 9977
Fax: 071 928 6539

Managed Derivatives magazine Mitre House, 44–46 Fleet St, London EC4Y 1BN, UK
Tel: 071 583 1347
Fax: 071 583 1728
Managing Editor: Beverly Chandler

The Managed Futures Association PO Box 287, Palo Alto, CA 94301, USA
Tel: 415 325 4533
Fax: 415 325 4944
Executive Director: Jane E. Martin

The National Futures Association 200, West Madison Street, Suite 1600, Chicago, Illinois 60606, USA
Tel: 312 781 1300
Fax: 312 781 1467
President: Robert Wilmouth

Rogers & Wells 58, Coleman Street, London EC2R 5BE, UK
Tel: 071 628 0101
Fax: 071 638 2008
Resident London partner: Eric Bettelheim

Rostron Parry 45–47 Clerkenwell Green, London EC1R, UK
Tel: 071 490 8062
Fax: 071 490 8063
Directors: Simon Rostron and John Parry

The Securities and Exchange Commission 450, Fifth Street NW, Washington DC 20549, USA
Tel: 202 272 7440
Fax: 202 272 7050
Information: Mary Hill

The Securities and Futures Authority Cottons Centre, Cottons Lane, London SE1 2QB, UK
Tel: 071 378 9000
Fax: 071 403 7569
Chief executive: Richard Farrant

The Securities and Investments Board Gavrelle House, 2–14, Bunhill Row, London EC1Y 8RA, UK
Tel: 071 638 1240
Fax: 071 382 5900
Information office: Clare Boyle

Simmons & Simmons 14, Dominion Street, London EC2M 2RJ, UK
Tel: 071 628 2020/071 528 9292
Fax: 071 588 4129/071 588 9418
Partner: Iain Cullen

Swiss Commodities, Futures and Options Association 11, Route de Drize, PO Box 1811, 1227 Geneva, Switzerland
Tel: 22 300 1967
Fax: 22 300 1970
Chairman: Paul-André Jacot

TASS Management Ltd. 40, Catherine Place, London SW1E 6HL, UK
Tel: 071 233 9797
Fax: 071 233 9159
Managing director: Nicola Meaden
Consultant: Stephanie Haworth

Glossary

This glossary does not just cover the derivatives industry jargon that may appear in the report, but endeavours to go beyond that and provide definitions of other names or phrases often used in derivatives.

At-the-market.   An Order to Buy or Sell at the Best Price at the Time that the Order is received.

At-the-money.   When the Strike Price of the Option is the Same as the Price of the Underlying Futures Contract.

Bear Spread.   The Sale of Near-month Futures Contracts against the Purchase of Deferred-month Contracts in the Hopes that the Price will Decline in the Near-month against the Further away Month.

Beta.   A Measure which Correlates Stock Price Movement to the Movement of an Index. It is used to Decide How Many Contracts are Required to Hedge an Index.

Bid.   To Buy a Number of Contracts at a Specific Price.

Broker.   Someone who Actually Trades in the Markets.

Bull Spread.   This is the Purchase of Near-month Futures Contracts against the Sale of Deferred-month Contracts in the Hope that the Price will Rise in the Near-month against the Further away Month.

Buy-on-the-close.   To Purchase a Contract at the End of a Trading Session at a Price within the Closing Range.

Buy-on-the-opening.   To Purchase a Contract at the Beginning of Trading Session at a Price within the Opening Range.

Call. The Period at the Opening or the Closing of the Market During which Futures Contract Prices are Established by Auction.

Call Option. A Contract Giving the Buyer the Right to Buy Something within a Specified Period of Time at a Specific Price.

Clearing-house. An Agency Associated with an Exchange which Guarantees all Trades, thus Assuring Contract Delivery and/or Financial Settlement.

Clearing Member. A Member of a Clearing-house Who is Responsible for Executing Client Trades. Clearing Members also Check on the Financial Strengths of Each of their Clients by Requiring Reports on Margins and Position.

The Close. The Time at the End of the Trading Session During which All Transactions are Considered to Have Been Made at 'the Close'. The Time is Officially Designated by the Exchange.

Commission. This has Various Meanings: The Fee which Clearing-houses Charge their Clients to Trade in Futures; The Fee that Brokers Charge their Clients; or the Introductory Fee Paid to an Intermediary who Puts one of his Clients into a Fund.

Commodity Trading Adviser. A CTA is a Person or Company who Analyses and Trades in the Futures and Options Markets.

Contract Month. The Month in which Futures Contracts may be Fulfilled by Taking or Making a Delivery.

Contrarian Theory. This is a Theory that the Majority Opinion about Market Trends is Wrong. A Contrarian will do the Opposite to the General Consensus of Opinion.

A Covered Position. This is a Trade which has been Offset by an Opposite and Equal Transaction.

Delivery. The Actual Physical Delivery of a Commodity in Fulfilment of a Futures Contract.

Delivery Month. The Month Specified in the Terms of a Futures Contract, During which Delivery may be Made.

Delta. This is the Factor Between the Fluctuation of a Futures Price and the Change in Premium for the Option on that Futures Contract. Deltas Change Constantly as the Option Premium Changes.

Discretionary Accounts. This is an Arrangement Whereby the Account-holder gives Complete Power to his or her Broker to Buy or Sell at the Broker's Discretion. Also Known as a Managed Account.

Discretionary Trader. Someone who Makes his or her Final Trading Decisions Personally, not Based upon Just Technical or Fundamental Analysis.

Even Up. To Close Out, Liquidate, or Cover an Open Position.

Financial Future. A Future on a Financial Commodity Such as Interest Rates, Currencies or Indexes.

Forward Contract. This is a Contract Between Two Parties who Agree to Buy or Sell a Specified Commodity in the Future. This is Different from a Futures Contract because in that Instance the Two Participants are Working Through a Clearing Corporation, not Directly With Each Other.

Fundamental Analysis. This is Analysis Based on the Effects of Specific Underlying Factors Such as Wars, Governmental Changes and the Like, on Supply and Demand and Market Prices.

Futures Contract. An Agreement to Purchase or Sell a Certain Amount of a Certain Commodity at a Time and Place Specified at the Outset at a Price Which is Agreed at the Outset.

Hedging. This is a Process through Which the Risk of Loss Due to Adverse Price Movements is Transferred using the Futures Markets.

In-the-money. This is an Options Expression Applying to a Call Option When the Strike Price is Below the Price of the Underlying Futures Contract. These Types of Options are the Most Expensive Because the Premium Covers Intrinsic Value as Well as Time Value.

Intrinsic Value. This is the Value of an Option Measured by the Difference Between the Strike Price and the Market Price of the Underlying Futures Contract when the Option is in-the-money (see above).

Leverage. In Europe, This is Usually Known as Gearing. It is the Relationship Between the Assets Under Management and Their Exposure in the Markets. The Easiest Metaphor is That of Using a Small Amount of Effort to Move a Larger Amount. It is the Proverbial Double-edged Sword.

Long. Buying a Futures Contract in Expectation of a Price Increase.

Margin. The Amount of Money Paid as Deposit on Futures.

Margin Call. This is the Call for More Funds to be Paid to Maintain Cover of a Margin.

Offer. This is the Opposite of a Bid. The Offer is an Offer to Sell at a Given Price.

The Opening. The Period at the Beginning of a Trading Session During which All Trades are Considered to have been Made at the Opening. The Exact Period is Specified by the Exchange.

Open Outcry.   The Method of Trading on the Floor of an Exchange which Involves Traders Standing in Pits and Literally Shouting at Each Other to Get the Best Deal on Price.

Option.   This is a One-sided Contract which Gives the Buyer the Right to Buy or Sell a Commodity at a Specified Price Within a Specified Time Period.

Out-of-the-money.   This is an Options Expression Referring to Call Options when the Strike Price is Above the Price of the Underlying Futures Contract or Put Options when the Strike Price is Below the Price of the Underlying Futures Contract.

Premium.   This is the Price Paid to Purchase an Option.

Put.   A Put Option is a Contract that Reserves the Right to Sell Something at a Specified Price within a Certain Period of Time.

Short.   To Sell a Futures Contract.

Spot.   The Spot Price of a Commodity is its Cash Market Price.

Straddle.   This is a Term Used in Futures Trading and is the Same as a Spread.

Strike Price.   This is the Specified Price at which an Option Contract can be Exercised.

Technical Analysis.   Analysis Based on the Uses of Charts and Computers to Examine Historic Fluctuations in Prices and Volumes in an Attempt to Predict Trends.

Directory of Europe's Futures and Options Exchanges

AUSTRIA

OTOB Clearing Bank AG Strauchgasse 1–3, Postbox 192, A-1014 Vienna, Austria
Tel:0222 531 650
Fax:0222 532 9740/531 65140

Products
Stock options on five Austrian blue chip stocks (CAV,EVN,OMV,Verbund and Wienerberger). Options and futures on the Austrian Traded Index (ATX) and Austrian government bond futures.

BELGIUM

Belgian Futures & Options Exchange Palais de la Bourse, Rue Henri Maus 2, 1000 Brussels, Belgium
Tel: 2 512 80 40
Fax: 2 513 83 42

Products
Futures on Belgian Government Bonds, BEL-20 Index, BIB and BGB. Stock options, index options (BXO) and index futures (BXF).

DENMARK

Futop The Copenhagen Stock Exchange and the Guarantee Fund for Danish Options and Futures, Kompagnistraede 15, Box 2017, DK-1012, Copenhagen K, Denmark
Tel: 3393 3311
Fax: 3393 4980

Products
Futures on the KFX Stock Index, mortgage bonds, Danish government bonds and bullet loans. Options on the KFX Stock Index Futures, Danish Government Bonds Futures, bullet loans and Danish stock futures.

FINLAND

Finnish Options Market Keskuskatu 7, 3rd Floor, Box 926, SF 00101, Helsinki, Finland
Tel: 358 0 131211
Fax: 358 0 13121211

Products
Futures on the FOX index, and futures on stocks and currencies Options on the FOX index and currencies.

FRANCE

Monep (Marché des Options Negociables de Paris) Societé de Compensation des Marchés Conditionnels-SCMC, 39 Rue Cambon, 75001 Paris, France

Products
Options on 27 equities, the CAC 40 short and long-term index.

Matif 176, Rue Montmartre, 75002 Paris, France
Tel: 1 40 28 82 82
Fax: 1 40 28 80 01

Products
Futures on the Ecu bond, notional bond, French treasury bond, 3-month Pibor, CAC 40 index, coffee robusta, white sugar and potatoes. Options on the Ecu bond, notional bond, 3-month Pibor, French medium-term futures and French treasury bonds.

GERMANY

DTB Deutsche Terminborse Grueneburgweg 102, D-60076 Frankfurt am Main I, Germany
Tel: 69 153030
Fax: 69 303 221

Products
Futures on DTB Bund, DTB DAX and medium-term notional bond. Options on equities and stocks, DAX index, DAX index futures Bund and medium-term Bund.

IRELAND (the Republic of)

The Irish Futures & Options Exchange Segrave House, Earlsfort Terrace, Dublin 2, Eire
Tel: 1 6767 413
Fax: 1 6614 645

Products
Long and short gilt futures, futures on Dibor and Iseq.

ITALY

Mercato Italiano Futures Comitato di Gestione Mercato Secondario dei titoli di stato, Piazza del Gesu 49, 00186 Rome, Italy
Tel: 39 6 6767 211
Fax: 39 6 6767 250

Products
Futures on the Italian treasury bond, 8–10 year and 3.5–5 year contracts.

NETHERLANDS

Agricultural Futures Markets Amsterdam Postbus 252, 1000 AG Amsterdam, The Netherlands
Tel: 020 550 4390
Fax: 0202 623 9949

Products
Futures on live hogs, potatoes and piglets.

European Options Exchange Optiebeurs NV, PO Box 19164, 1000 GD
Amsterdam, The Netherlands
Tel: 31 20 550 4550
Fax: 31 20 623 0012

Products
Futures on the EOE index, Dutch Top 5 index, notional bond, the Eurotop
100 index and the US dollar. Options on equities, government bonds, EOE index,
MMI index, XMI Leaps, the dollar, the jumbo dollar, Dutch Top 5 index,
Eurotop 100 index, gold and the Guilder bond.

NORWAY

Oslo Stock Exchange PO Box 460 Sentrum, N-0105 Oslo, Norway
Tel: 47 22 341700
Fax: 47 22 416590

Products
Options on Bergesen, Saga Petroleum, Norsk Hydro, Hafslund Nycomed,
Kvcerner and OBX-index. Futures on OBX-index and interest rate futures on
government bond.

SPAIN

Meff Renta Fija (Exchange for bonds and interest rates) Via Laietana, 58, 08003
Barcelona, Spain
Tel: 343 412 1128
Fax: 343 268 4769

Meff Renta Variable (Exchange for equity derivatives) Torre Picasso, Planta
26, 28020 Madrid, Spain
Tel: 341 585 08 00
Fax: 341 571 95 42

Products
Futures on three year notional bond, ten year notional bond, 90 day Mibor,
Peseta/US dollar, Peseta/D-Mark, Ibex 35. Options on 90 day Mibor, three
year notional bond, ten year notional bond, Ibex 35, Mibor 90, Notional Bond
10% (three year), Notional Bond 10% (five year). Stock options (BBV, Endesa,
Repsol and Telefonica).

SWEDEN

OM Stockholm AB Box 16305, S 103 26 Stockholm, Sweden
Tel: 46 8 700 06 00
Fax: 46 8 723 10 92

Products
Futures on stocks, OMX Stock index, Treasury Bill futures, OMR2 interest rate
futures, OMR5 interest rate futures, OMR5 Government bond futures, OMR10
interest rate futures, SBAB5 interest rate futures, MBB2 Mortgage bond futures,
MBB5 interest rate futures, CT5 mortgage bond futures, CT2 interest rate
futures, CT5 interest rate futures, SB5 Mortgage bond futures, STIBOR 3
month. Options on stocks, OMX stock index, interest rate options, OMR5
Government bond options.

SWITZERLAND

Swiss Options & Financial Futures Exchange Ltd. (Soffex) Neumattstrasse 7,
CH-8953, Dietikon, Zurich, Switzerland
Tel: 1 740 3020
Fax: 1 741 1800

Products
Futures on the Swiss Market index, Swiss Government bonds. Options on the
Swiss Market index, stock options, low exercise price options (LEPO) and Equity
options.

UNITED KINGDOM

International Petroleum Exchange International House, 1, St Katharine's Way,
London E1 9UN, UK
Tel: 071 481 0643
Fax: 071 481 8485

Products
Futures on Brent Crude, gas oil, Unleaded gasoline. Options on Brent Crude
and gas oil.

London Commodity Exchange 1, Commodity Quay, St Katharine Docks,
London E1 9AX, UK
Tel: 071 481 2080
Fax: 071 702 9923

Products
Futures on robusta coffee, no.7 cocoa, no.7 premium raw sugar, no.5 white sugar, Freight index (Biffex), EC wheat, EC barley and potatoes. Options on robusta coffee, No.7 cocoa, No.5 white sugar, wheat, barley and potatoes.

London International Financial Futures and Options Exchange (Liffe) Cannon Bridge House, 1, Cousin Lane, London EC4R 3XX, UK
Tel: 071 623 0444
Fax: 071 588 3624

Products
Futures on FTSE 100 index, Spanish government bond, long gilt, German government bond(BUND and BOBL), Medium term German government bond, US treasury bond, Italian government bond, ECU bond, Japanese government bond, three-month Eurodollar, three-month Sterling, three-month Euromark, three-month Euroswiss, three-month ECU, three-month Eurolira. Options on three-month Sterling, three-month Eurodollar, three-month ECU, three-month Euroswiss, three-month Euromark, long gilt, German government bond, US treasury bond, Italian government bond, FTSE 100, equity options.

London Metal Exchange E Wing, 4th Floor, Plantation House, Fenchurch St, London EC3M 3AP, UK
Tel: 071 626 3311
Fax: 071 626 1703

Products
Futures on aluminium high grade 99.7%, copper grade A, lead 99.97%, nickel 99.80%, tin 99.85%, zinc special high grade 99.995%, secondary aluminium alloy ingot.

GLOBEX

Globex is an international electronic system for futures and options that will allow participating exchanges to list their products for trading on the system. The system has been developed by Reuters for use by the Chicago Mercantile Exchange (CME) and the Chicago Board of Trade (CBOT) and allows electronic trading of futures and options orders after the close of the exchanges' open outcry trading hours. The objective for Globex is that it will be accessible around the world and extend the exchanges' current trading days, allowing virtual around the clock trading.

Globex was launched in 1992 and involves the following exchanges: the CME, the CBOT and the Matif. The Matif is the most successful of the exchanges, representing 85% of the volume traded. Research undertaken by the Matif in September 1993, showing that CTAs and mutual funds among their members were increasingly turning to Globex, coincided with Globex's launch of a new marketing campaign.

Other exchanges have agreed, in principle, to join Globex but at the time of writing, no other negotiations are being held. Globex's talks with Liffe have not progressed because of questions over the exclusivity of offering a bund contract.

Index

Accounting principles 63
Arbitrage pricing theory 36
Austria
  exchange 183
  regulation 109

Belgium
  exchange 183
  regulation 110
  tax 151
Bolsa Mercadorias & de Futuros 8
Bonds vii
Bretton Woods 6

Capital adequacy 53
Chicago Board of Trade 4, 8
Chicago Mercantile Exchange 5, 8
Collective investment schemes ix
Commodities Corporation 17
Commodities Futures Trading
  Commission 18, 19, 144
Commodity pool operators 18, 35, 38
Commodity trading advisors 17, 35, 38
Commonwealth of Virginia 100
Conferences 81
Conti-Commodities 18
Currency forwards vii

Demographic change 49
Denmark
  exchange 184
  regulation 112
Derivative 3

Discretionary analysts 42
Donchian, Richard D. 17
Dunn & Hargitt 17

Equities vii
European financial newspapers 72
European Managed Futures
  Association 57, 171
European traders 31, 32

Fees 44, 58
Financial futures 6
Finland
  exchange 184
  regulation 114
Forex vii
Fortune 500 viii
France
  exchange 184
  regulation 115
  tax 153
Fundamental analysts 40
Futures vii, viii, 3, 11
Futures and Options Funds (Fofs) 101,
  137, 138

Geared Futures and Options Funds
  (Gfofs) 101, 137, 138
Gearing 13, 58
Germany
  exchange 185
  regulation 118
  tax 154

Gibraltar
   regulation   139
Globex   188
Glossary   179
Greece
   regulation   121
Group of Thirty Report   8
Guaranteed funds   37, 38, 95
Guernsey
   regulation   141

Hedging   vii

Indexes   55
Index funds   viii
Ireland
   exchange   185
   regulation   121
Isle of Man
   regulation   140
Italy
   exchange   185
   regulation   124

Japan
   regulation   148
Jersey
   regulation   141

Kookyer, William   18
Kovner, Bruce   18

Lintner, John   24
London Clearing House   5
London Commodities Exchange   5
London International Financial Futures
   Exchange (Liffe)   ix, 5, 8, 187
London Metal Exchange   5, 8
Luxembourg
   regulation   126
   tax   155

Managed Account Reports (Mar)   20,
   25, 30
Managed futures   3, 19
Managed Futures Association   60
Managed futures funds   viii, 35
Marcus, Michael   18
Margin payments   13
Market wizards   42

Markowitz, Harry   21, 23
Matif   8, 184
Miller, Merton   21, 23
Modern Portfolio Theory   23
Multi-adviser funds   36

Netherlands, The
   exchange   185
   regulation   128
   tax   155
Norway
   exchange   186
   regulation   130
Nymex   8

Options   vii, viii, 3, 11
Origins of the Industry   3
Osaka   8
Over-the-Counter   8

Pension Consultants   52
Peters, Carl   26
Portugal
   regulation   131
   tax   159
Press relations   71
Private pools   ix, 18
Property   vii

Quantitative investment   vi

Rate of return   58
Risk of ruin   58
Royal Exchange   5

Samuelson, Paul   18
Securities and Exchange
   Commission   19
Semi-deviation   58
Sharpe ratio   59
Sharpe, William   21, 23
Shearson Lehman Brothers   17
Size of managed futures industry   18
Spain
   exchange   186
   regulation   132
   tax   159
Standard deviation   58
Sweden
   exchange   187
   regulation   133

Switzerland
    exchange   187
    regulation   135
    tax   159
Swops   vii
Sydney Futures Exchange   8

Technical analysts   41
Tiffe   8
To arrive contracts   4
Track records   53, 73
Trading managers   51, 59

Trustees rules   165

Ucits   106, 167
United Kingdom
    exchange   187
    regulation   136
    tax   160
United States of America
    regulation   143
Useful contacts   171

Worst ever drawdown   58